ETERNALLY YOURS

God's Greatest Gift to Mankind

| NUMBERS |

RABBI REUVEN MANN

Copyright © 2020 Reuven Mann
Published by: Observant Artist Community Circle, Inc.
All rights reserved.

Dedication

This book is dedicated to the memory of Rabbi Mark Blumkin, Mordechai Boaz Ben Avraham Yosef of blessed memory, who was a unique individual with a thirst for knowledge and a passionate desire to plumb the depths of Torah's concepts. Upon retirement from his job at the I.R.S. at the age of 66, he joined our Torah academy, Yeshiva B'nei Torah, for full time study. He felt fully comfortable learning with others who were many years his junior. His enthusiasm for learning was a source of great inspiration for all the talmidei HaYeshiva. He studied diligently at the Yeshiva for 22 years, and received Smicha at the age of 80.

He was a humble and compassionate person who was concerned for the welfare of all people. He bore the sufferings of his illness without complaint, was always positive and upbeat, and profusely thankful for the joy he received from those who came to visit and study with him. May his memory be a blessing and source of inspiration for his family, friends and all who knew him.

In loving memory,

Doris Blumkin

Yaakov and Ilana Melohn

Joseph and Malka Melohn
Alexander, Don and Kate

Avi Melohn

Meir Melohn

Moshe and Brynde Rieder
Chana, Aryeh and Aharon

Baruch and Sarah Muehlgay

Miriam Melohn

Isaac Melohn

Rabbi Israel Chait, Dean
Rabbi Reuven Mann, Menahel Emeritus
The Rabbis and Students of Yeshiva B'nei Torah

Dedication

This book is dedicated to Jules Glogower, Yehudah ben Yehoshua Halevi, *zichrono livracha*, a modest and honest individual who was very meticulous in his tefillot. A clinical psychologist, blessed with deep insights into the human personality, he was a wise and loving adviser to family, friends and those in need. He faced life's challenges with humor, a calm disposition and clarity of thought. May his memory continue to inspire all who knew him.

And to his loving wife of 69 years, Janet Glogower, Sprinza bat Harav Issacher Dov, *zichrona livracha*, a humble, soft spoken woman whose perfection of character was reflected in the purity of her speech and clarity of her thought.
She devoted her life to raising her family with great love and kindness, in accordance with the letter of Torah law and its objective.
Her interactions with friends, acquaintances and even strangers were always characterized by "*seiver panim yafot*," a friendly and cheerful countenance. May her memory continue to inspire those who knew her.

In loving memory,

The Glogower family

Dedication

This book is also dedicated to the memory of our parents:

Yetta and Harry Mann, *zichronam livracha*, who always emphasized, by word and deed, the supreme importance of learning Torah, getting a good education and being a good Jew.

Sari and Herman Jakob, *zicronam livracha*, who emerged from the concentration camps to rebuild their lives, raise a family and renew their dedication to Judaism, Israel and the Jewish People.

And to our aunt, Blanka Hermann, *zichrona livracha*, who survived Auschwitz and rebuilt her life in Sydney, Australia. She was a kind and charitable woman who had a great love for the Jewish People and Eretz Yisrael.

In loving memory,

Rabbi and Rebbetzin Reuven Mann

Acknowledgements

The articles in this book were written over the course of the last nine years. I began writing a weekly piece on the Parsha when I began my tenure as Rabbi of the Young Israel of Phoenix, Arizona. I would like to thank Maxine Blecher, who was the Synagogue Secretary, for her assistance in this endeavor. At that time (before I became a user of the iPad), I wrote the articles in longhand and she was able to read them and type them up. We reviewed each column and her feedback contributed to the quality of the writing.

About seven and a half years ago Devora Krischer, who had been a professional editor for Jewish publications, volunteered to perform that service for me. She had the essential qualification of being able to read my handwriting but more importantly applied her great editing skills to my compositions. Her insights and suggestions proved to be a great asset in enhancing the literary quality of my work.

Devora is a kind, caring and devoted woman who is always there to be helpful and contribute her substantial skills to the needs of the Jewish community. She continues to review and edit my weekly Torah essays with her characteristic enthusiasm and good cheer. I thank her and wish her good health and all of Hashem's blessings for many, many years.

This book is the brainchild of my student, Rabbi Richard Borah, who thought it would be a good idea to collect my *Dvar Torahs* (Torah articles) and present them as a book for the Jewish and general public. He put in a great deal of work discharging the many tasks necessary to organize the publication of a book. He is himself the author of two works, "Man as Prime Mover: A Torah Perspective on Contemporary

Philosophy and Science" and "The Rambam & The Rav On The 54 Portions of The Torah."

I have greatly enjoyed our friendship and intellectual relationship, which goes back a long way. I wish him and his wife Andrea great happiness and *nachat* (satisfaction) from their beautiful children as well as Hashem's blessings in all that they do.

Another student of mine, Rabbi Marshall Gisser, contributed his formidable skills to this book. He is an extremely talented graphic artist who is responsible for the front and back covers. I believe that Torah should be presented in a manner that is beautiful in both form and content. The aesthetics of a *sefer* (religious work) are important to me and Rabbi Gisser's efforts enabled that aspect of the work to be very appealing. His life is dedicated to the dissemination of Torah which he does via his writings on his website, Mesora.org. This resource provides great Torah teachings of Rabbi Gisser and numerous other Rabbis, and reaches thousands of people many of whom have been brought closer to Judaism as a result. May Rabbi Gisser continue to advance in his study and teaching of Torah and merit Hashem's blessings in all his endeavors.

Estee Lichter joined our editorial team to participate in the preparation of *Eternally Yours* on Genesis. Both she and her husband Joey have been students of mine for twenty-five years. I remember with great fondness the many learning sessions, Torah discussions and great Shabbat and Holiday meals we shared together. Estee exudes great enthusiasm and palpable love of Torah study. She is an extremely talented writer, editor and eagle-eyed proofreader. When I asked her to be part of the team, she responded by thanking me for the opportunity. Her dedication to removing any flaws the book might have and improving its presentation and clarity is boundless. She has characterized her work as a *labor of love*. I consider myself fortunate to count Estee and Joey among my students and hope to enjoy our relationship for many years. May they derive great joy from their wonderful children and *nachat* from all that they do.

Finally, I would like to acknowledge the unique role my wife Linda has played in my life. Without her, I could not have spent my time immersed in learning, teaching, and providing guidance and counseling to individuals and married couples. Being *Menahel* (educational director) of Yeshiva B'nei Torah as well as a community Rabbi consumed virtually all of my time. In addition, students and congregants were a regular feature of Shabbat and Yom Tov meals, and, due to Linda's great cooking and hosting skills, our home became the "invitation" of choice.

Linda is a very wise, determined, and capable woman whose dedication to our life's mission of disseminating Torah was absolutely vital to any success we achieved. Whoever feels gratitude to me for any way in which I benefited them must be equally thankful to her for she made it all possible. May she be blessed with good health and long years, *nachat* from children and grandchildren, and fulfillment of her dream of spending much more time in *Eretz Yisrael*.

From the Author

My entire career, which spans over forty years, has been dedicated to the dissemination of Torah Judaism in the settings of the classroom, *Beit Medrash* and Synagogue. As a Rebbe, I have taught a number of subjects including Talmud, *Chumash* (The Five Books of Moses), *Tanach* (scripture) and *Hashkafa* (philosophy). My objective as a teacher was to penetrate to the depths of the classical Jewish texts (to the best of my abilities) and demonstrate how the ideas of Torah are Divine, and, therefore, timeless and relevant to all of life's challenges.

My method of teaching was *not* to deliver lectures to my students. My classes are best described as *interactive*. I would generate a *participatory* analysis of the subject matter and encourage my students to ask the pertinent questions and try their hands at formulating meaningful answers. My goal was not to merely transmit information and concepts, but to train the students to internalize the unique methodology which would enable them to become Torah scholars in their own right.

Through the years, a particular love and fascination of mine was the study of *Chumash*. The subject matter therein is often presented in a *cryptic* manner. The profound ideas embedded in the narratives and other sections of the Chumash lie hidden beneath the surface and, just as in Talmud, one must learn to navigate its "stormy seas" and extract its "buried" treasures.

Rabbi Chanina said, "I have learned much from my teachers, more from my colleagues and most of all from my students" (Talmud Taanis 7a). I have been fortunate to learn from wonderful teachers. In addition to the great Talmudic

Masters who taught at the Rabbi Isaac Elchanon Theological Seminary (Yeshiva University) during the 1960s, I also had the privilege to hear magnificent shiurim from the master, *Moreinu* (Our Teacher) Hagaon Rabbi Joseph Soloveitchik ZT"L. He was a genius of towering proportions in *all* areas of Torah knowledge whose ability to elucidate complicated ideas in the clearest and most compelling manner was *legendary*.

When I was a student "sitting at the feet" of these great Torah scholars, my goal was not just to understand and absorb the content of what they were teaching. I also sought to grasp their method of thinking and the special approach which enabled them to reach their brilliant conclusions. I was most focused on incorporating their *method of learning* and developed a technique which I call "listening with the third ear" (borrowed from the title of a book by the famous psychoanalyst Theodore Reik). This enabled me to observe their thinking patterns and study how they would maneuver through the complicated material and arrive at their penetrating *halachic* formulations.

I also had the good fortune to meet and become close friends with Rabbi Israel Chait, *Shlita*. He was a student of Rav Soloveitchik whom I regard as a great intellect and master of the *Brisker Method* (a conceptual method of Talmudic analysis). We would learn *bechavruta* (learning partners) and these sessions provided a great opportunity to advance my understanding and application of the *Brisker* approach.

In 1971, Rabbi Chait and I established Yeshiva B'nei Torah, where I served as *Menahel* (educational director) and *Maggid Shiur* (Instructor of Talmud) for almost forty years. The intellectual atmosphere in this great place was intense and unique. I was always surrounded by formidable students who had a seemingly insatiable desire for knowledge and understanding and were trained and encouraged to ask the most daunting questions.

A great benefit of being in the Yeshiva was the opportunity it provided to hear the special presentations in Chumash given by Rabbi Chait. These were masterpieces of analysis and conceptualization of the Bible narratives. He would take apart a narrative and analyze the pertinent *Midrashim* and commentaries, in order to flesh out the deeper ideas of the stories. He delivered *breakthrough* discourses on numerous areas. Rabbi Chait was able to derive the philosophical principles that were at the heart of the Biblical stories and demonstrate how we can extract fundamental ideas, relevant to all areas of life by a proper understanding of the Chumash.

Many of the ideas and approaches I incorporated in the following essays were inspired by elucidations I heard from Rabbi Chait. I take this opportunity to express to him my great gratitude for all his friendship, teaching, personal advice and assistance, in so many areas over the years. May Hashem grant him good health and strength to be able to continue his masterful teaching and personal guidance to all who seek it, for many, many years.

I have tried to utilize the approach outlined above in all of the many Chumash classes I have given over the years. I have taught male students at Yeshiva B'nei Torah, female students at Masoret: Institute of Advanced Judaic Studies for Women (which I and Rabbi Daniel Rosenthal founded in 1993), and to men and women at the various Synagogues at which I served as Rabbi, over the years (they include: Jewish Community Center of Inwood, Rinat Yisrael Of Plainview N.Y. and Young Israel of Phoenix, Arizona).

Most of the ideas contained in this book were worked out in creative sessions with the intellectually energetic students I have been fortunate to have. For the past ten years, I have written a weekly column on the Parsha of the week. A student of mine, Rabbi Richard Borah, suggested that we organize these writings and compile them in a book for the benefit of others who might find them useful and interesting. Rabbi Borah has been a great help in the many tasks that must be accomplished before a book can "see the light of day."

I have utilized the classical sources such as the Midrashim, Rashi, Rambam, Ramban, Sforno, Ibn Ezra, Ralbag, Abarbanel, Malbim, Rabbi Samson Raphael Hirsch, Rabbi Joseph B. Soloveitchik, and many others. My goal was not to merely repeat what they say, but to analyze, clarify and make sense of their words and show how they enable us to elucidate the text.

The Nature and Purpose of This Book

This book contains essays on every one of the *Parshas* that comprise the Book of Numbers. In them, I seek to raise penetrating questions that get to the heart of the story, and to decipher them to extract their deeper meaning.

My conviction is that the Torah is from God and is therefore eternally relevant. My goal is to discover the underlying ideas and philosophy outlined for us in God's *own* Book. Beyond that, I seek to show how Divine teachings are germane to the issues and problems we face today as individuals and a society.

I have striven to write the articles in a clear, lucid, and compelling manner. It is extremely important to me that the reader find the essays *interesting* and enjoyable, as well as educational and inspiring.

I hope that this book will be of value to ordinary laymen as well as rabbis and teachers, by raising many challenging and original questions and resolutions. The philosophy it reflects is scrupulously based on classical Orthodox Jewish theology.

The material in this book can stimulate spirited discussion and creative thinking and help foster a greater interest in the study of *Chumash*. Although I have written the book from the perspective of a rabbi, I believe it will appeal to those who are not religious and to gentiles as well.

By dealing with the major life challenges of a personal and social nature that we all confront, this book offers insights that are meant to *enrich* the mind and heart.

It is my hope that this book will enhance the reader's enjoyment and appreciation of Torah. I believe it will be of interest to the "ordinary" reader as well as to teachers and pulpit Rabbis, because it will stimulate thought and provide ideas and interpretations that will be worthy of analysis and discussion.

My greatest hope is that it will engender interest in and enjoyment of the study of Torah. I have referred to Torah, in the subtitle, as "God's greatest gift to mankind." That has been the guiding principle of my life, and I now seek to share that with you.

It is unfortunate that many Jews do not look at it that way. It is my prayer that this work will make a contribution, however modest, to rectifying that situation.

Rabbi Reuven Mann, March 2020

Note to Reader:

The Book of Bamidbar is divided into 10 sections called Parshas or Sedras. Beginning in late spring, around the time of the Festival of Shavuot, each one is read aloud to the congregation in Synagogues, one per week, on the Sabbath. The last two Parshas, Matot and Masei, are sometimes read individually, but, depending on the calendar, may be read on the same week, in a so-called "double Parsha." After Bamidbar is completed, the reading of Deuteronomy begins.

Every Parsha has a Hebrew name, usually derived from one of the words in its first or second verse. The First Parsha, or Sedra, is Bamidbar. Bamidbar translates as "In the Desert." The second Parsha is Naso, which means "Take a Census." Then comes Beha'alotcha, "When You Kindle (the Lamps)", on through Shelah, "Send out," and Korach (the Hebrew name of Korah), and so on.

Throughout the book, Hebrew terminology, when used, is italicized and, upon its first use, is followed by a translation. All terms are again translated in the glossary, which can be found at the end of the book.

Table of Contents

Acknowledgements..i
From the Author..iv
Note to Reader...ix

Introduction..4
BAMIDBAR
Significance of a Census...16
You Were There...19
Were We Coerced?...22
Torah is Freedom...26

NASO
The Vindicated Adulteress..32
Reverence for the Soul...37
Sins of the Scholars...42
Spiritual Dining...47

BEHA'ALOTCHA
The True Leader..52
Was Jethro Selfish?..56
Jews By Choice...60
Judaism Must Inspire Unity and Love..............................64
Rebellion in the Wilderness......................................69

SHELACH
The Sin of the Spies: Excessive Guilt 78
Absolute Faith in Hashem's Promise 83
The Spies 86
Sin of the Spies 91

KORACH
Korachism 96
What a Difference a Friend Makes 100
Popularity is Ephemeral 104
The Hidden Blessing Within the Curse 108
The True Teachers of Torah 112
Rebellion 118

CHUKAT
Vicarious Atonement? 124
In the Merit of the Righteous 128
Do We Respect Other Religions? 131
The Red Heifer 136
Death by the Kiss 140

BALAK
Seduction 146
Those Who Curse 151
We Are Different! 154
The Power of a Curse 158

PINCHAS
Indifference of the Righteous 164

Religious Zealots 169
The Hedonism of the Times 172
The Righteous Zealot 176
Righteous Revenge 180
A Prophet of Their Own 184
Why Did Elijah Despair? 189

MATOT-MASEI

Dealing with Chutzpah 196
Fatal Attraction 200
Mean What You Say 204
Excessive Religiosity 208
Sometimes Anger Works 212
Judaism is the Answer 216

Glossary 220

Introduction

Bamidbar: The Book of Failure and Hope

Part I: Doom in the Desert

Bamidbar, the fourth Book of the Torah, begins at a propitious moment in Jewish history, the second year after the great redemption from Egypt. Much had transpired during that time: the nation had "encountered" God on Mount Sinai and received His Torah.

The Israelites then remained encamped around the mountain for a year, because there was much to accomplish. They had to study the Torah and learn to perform the *mitzvot* (commandments). In addition, the nation was preoccupied with building the *Mishkan* (Tabernacle), the precursor to the Holy Temple in Jerusalem.

The year had been marked by an especially grievous calamity. The sin of the Golden Calf was one of the worst in Jewish history, bringing the nation to the precipice of destruction. Fortunately, Moses' prayerful intervention saved the day and the people resumed their tasks. In the second year after the Exodus, the dedication of the *Mishkan* was complete, and all preparations were made for the conquest and settlement of the Land that God had promised Abraham to give to his children.

The Book of Bamidbar begins on a certain high note. One can sense Moses' enthusiasm as he entreats his father-in-law, Jethro, to join the people in settling Israel so he can partake of all the blessings that Hashem has in store for the Jews.

However, Moses' initial excitement did not endure. The Book of Bamidbar, which was supposed to be filled with glory and accomplishment, turned out to be the saddest and most disappointing in the entire Torah.

It did not take long for a spirit of rebelliousness to break out. We read about the revolt over food, with the people complaining about the monotony of the *manna*. (See "The True Leader," page 42, and "Rebellion in the Wilderness," page 59). This brought forth a severe punishment from God. Why, at this point, did the people see fit to complain about their diet? Did the sudden outbreak of discontent manifest an underlying anxiety about the imminent invasion of Canaan?

One might think so, because the Book of Bamidbar is dominated by the tragic incident of the Spies. In response to Moses' injunction to "go up and conquer" (Deuteronomy 1:21), the people asked to send men on a mission to scout out the land and return with a report about their findings.

This turned out to be a disaster, because the Spies infected the people with extreme panic about the might of the land's inhabitants. (See "The Sin of the Spies: Excessive Guilt," page 66, and "The Spies," page 73). God responded with His decree that the conquest of the land would be postponed for 40 years, until the entire generation of adults who had left Egypt passed away. This development converted Bamidbar into a Book of sadness and failure.

The terrible decree further impacted the people in that it generated a series of rebellions. Most outrageous was that of Korah and his "congregation," who openly plotted to derail Moses' religious authority. Korah sought to overturn Moses' appointment of Aaron as the Kohain and the Levite Tribe as the administrators of the Temple.

It is important to note that Korah's rebellion and the debacle of the Spies were the work of distinguished, national leaders. Only Hashem's providential intervention enabled Moses to retain his authority and control over the nation. But he was continuously challenged by the insubordination of discontented personalities.

Bamidbar illustrates that, indeed, even our greatest leaders are subject to sin. In this Book, we learn about the transgressions of Moses' sister, Miriam, and his brother, Aaron. Incomprehensibly, she "complained" that Moses had separated from his wife (Rashi on Numbers 12:1). He had done so at God's behest, because he had reached the highest level of prophecy, and had to be constantly ready for divine communication. However, Miriam was not aware of this, and her criticism was deemed to be inappropriate.

The rebellious spirit of the people eventually took its toll on Moses and Aaron, and they stumbled. When the people complained about the absence of water, God told Moses and Aaron to "*speak* to the rock, that it give forth its waters" (Numbers 20:8). Inexplicably, Moses *hit* the rock, and Hashem regarded this as a failure to sanctify His Name in the midst of the Congregation.

The punishment was harsh and irrevocable. Moses, who had led the Jews out of Egypt, brought down the Torah from Mount Sinai and guided the Israelites on their trek through the Wilderness, would not complete the mission by leading them in their glorious conquest of the Land.

The Book of Bamidbar contains many other sad stories, such as the encounter with the wicked Balaam. It is true that God thwarted his desire to utter "curses" against the Jewish people. However, this evil "prophet" left his mark, as Jewish males fell prey to his nefarious scheme of entrapment. Balaam advised the women of Moab to use sexual seduction to lure the Jewish men into the worship of the idol *Peor* (see "Religious Zealots," page 180.) This trespass was so egregious that it caused a plague, leading to the death of 24,000 people.

Part II: Greatness of Spirit

While there is much that is of a negative character in Bamidbar, that is not the Book's total story. Alongside of the failures we have recounted, there are episodes of spiritual grandeur.

Prior to the first anniversary of the Exodus, Moses commanded the Nation to bring the Passover Sacrifice on the 14th of Nissan in accordance with all its "Statutes and Judgements" (Numbers 9:3). Among its requirements is the rule that anyone in a state of ritual impurity, because of contact with a corpse, is disqualified from performing this *mitzvah* (commandment). According to Jewish law, a person who fails to fulfill a commandment because of circumstances beyond his control bears no guilt before God.

In spite of that dispensation, a group of such "impure" people came before Moses and implored him to be given another opportunity, at a time when they would have become ritually pure, to bring the Passover offering. Moses inquired of God, who responded by establishing the Law of the "Second Passover," which commands all who were unable (or unwilling) to offer the Passover on its initial date to do so at an alternative time (the 14th of the Hebrew month of *Iyar*).

Let us recognize the nobility of spirit which motivated these "impure" people to issue their request. They would have suffered no consequences for failure to perform the ritual, so what was it that motivated their plea?

Apparently, these people recognized and appreciated the great spiritual benefits afforded by fulfillment of the Commandments, especially the Passover, whose central theme is the renunciation of Idolatry. Moreover, they understood how fundamental this particular *mitzvah* is to the Jewish People as a commemoration of the Exodus. They did not want to be prevented from bonding with their brothers and sisters in this great experience.

This expression of commitment to Torah and the Jewish People represents a high point in the history of the Jews.

Greatness of spirit can also be seen in the interaction between Moses and the representatives of the tribes of Reuben and Gad. Moses had conquered the land on the Eastern side of the Jordan. (See "Dealing with Chutzpah, page 174). This territory contained vast expanses of rich pasture which was perfectly suited for these tribes, who had large holdings of livestock. They requested that Moses allow them to forfeit their portion on the Western side of the Jordan and instead take their inheritance on this newly acquired area. Upon hearing this, Moses became furious and lashed out, accusing them of repeating the crime of the Spies, who induced the national panic that halted the forward march to Israel.

The leaders of the two tribes got the message. They offered to be in the vanguard of the invading forces and lead the battle for the Promised Land. They would remain with their brothers until the land of Israel was conquered and settled. Only then would they return to their families on the other side of the Jordan.

An agreement was struck between the parties and peace was preserved. Subsequently, the two tribes fulfilled all their guarantees. They fought at the head of their brothers for 14 years until the conquest was complete. The ability of the people to rise above partisan interests and work out viable compromises that retained national unity reflects a high level of idealism and commitment which should motivate and inspire us today.

Part III: Rectification of Sin

Beyond the stories recorded in Bamidbar, a number of new Commandments are revealed by Moses in this Book. In addition to *Second Passover* they include *Sotah*, *Nazir*, *Tzitzit* (fringes on garments), *Red Heifer*, *Purging of Vessels* and more.

One may rightfully ask, is there a connection between the *Mitzvot* detailed here and the narratives communicated in this Book? What philosophical relevance do these religious imperatives have to the moral themes of the stories we read here?

Addressing these questions necessarily entails a bit of speculation, but I would like to put forth a certain hypothesis. As I see it, the narratives of Bamidbar are primarily about the failures and setbacks experienced by the Jews on their journey to God's land. Thus, we must ask, what is the teaching of the Torah on the subject of man's *defeats* in the *Milchemet HaChaim* (the "Battle of Life")?

I would like to suggest that it is that we are never to be broken by our inability to attain our goals or live up to our standards of moral excellence. While Bamidbar is a Book of failure, it is also one of hope, because Judaism is rooted in the doctrine of the *perfectibility of man* and of mankind.

Many of the Commandments in Bamidbar are based on the idea of correcting defects and *repairing sin*. They presuppose that man is prone to failure, but, that he can overcome it. The Torah prescribes corrective measures to transform weaknesses into strengths, flaws into capabilities. Setbacks can become the catalyst for growth and progress.

For example, the institution of *Nazir* consists of a vow to abstain from wine, not cut one's hair, and avoid any contact with a corpse. This is a completely voluntary *mitzvah*, as no one is obligated to become a *Nazirite*.

In general, Judaism eschews asceticism and favors disciplined and moderate gratification of one's desires, and this seems to be at odds with the suppression of bodily pleasure symbolized by the restrictions incumbent on a Nazir. However, sometimes a person goes to extremes of indulgence and needs to be weaned of his excesses. It might then be wise to take upon himself, for a limited amount of time, a vow of abstention. This temporary extreme of self-denial will allow him to regain his moral equilibrium. The *mitzvah* of *Nazirut* guides a person who has allowed himself to get caught up in a hedonistic lifestyle to find his way back to the intelligent and moderate pathway of Torah. (See "Reverence for the Soul" on page 33).

Another theme expressed in Bamidbar's *Mitzvot* is that of *purification* from sin and rebirth of the personality. Judaism asserts that man is a sinner by nature (although it vehemently rejects the notion that he is *evil* by nature). Because of this very nature, our path to perfection inevitably entails foolishness and irrational behaviors. However, the Creator also implanted in man the ability to recognize failures and overcome them.

It is therefore not by accident that the Commandment of the *Red Heifer* and that of *Purging of Vessels* make their appearance here. The former is concerned with man's purification from the *tumah* (spiritual impurity) he acquires from his encounter with a dead body. The latter teaches that a vessel which has become ritually tainted by absorption of unkosher substances can be cleansed of those elements and once again become functional.

So too can the human personality expunge the negative attitudes and dispositions it has internalized, to become a new and better person. In fact, that is precisely what God did in response to the sin of the Spies. The decree of a 40-year trek in the wilderness was not exclusively a punishment. It was intended as an experience of training and growth. The Rambam explains, "It was the result of God's wisdom that the Israelites were led about in the wilderness till they acquired courage. For it is a well-known fact that traveling in the wilderness and privation of bodily enjoyments such as bathing, produce courage, while the reverse is the source of faintheartedness; besides another generation arose during the wandering that had not been accustomed to degradation and slavery"(Guide for the Perplexed, part 3, chapter 32).

Thus, in the book of Bamidbar, the Torah merges narratives of setbacks and rebellions with Commandments that pertain to man's ability to rectify his transgressions and renew his spirit. The Torah is very optimistic about man's ability to overcome sin and attain perfection.

Part IV: A World Redeemed

Despite the ominous events that seem to mark Bamidbar as a book of tragedy, Bamidbar may be rightly described as the Book of both *failure and hope*. That is because it emerges that the Jews are an *eternal* People.

In the words of the Rambam, "We are in possession of a divine assurance that Israel is indestructible and imperishable, and will always continue to be a preeminent community. As it is impossible for God to cease to exist, so is Israel's destruction and disappearance from the world unthinkable, as we read, 'For I the Lord change not, and you, O sons of Jacob, will not be consumed' (Malachi 3:6). Similarly He has avowed and assured us that it is unimaginable that He will reject us entirely even if we disobey Him, and disregard His behests, as the prophet Jeremiah avers, 'Thus says the Lord: If heaven above can be measured, and the foundations of the earth searched out beneath, then will I also cast off all the seed of Israel for all that they have done, says the Lord' (Jeremiah 31:36)." (Rambam's "Epistle to Yemen," in A Maimonides Reader by Isadore Twersky [1972], p.445).

However, this assurance should not give rise to a sense of complacency or reduction of energy in pursuit of our national spiritual goals. For God will not miraculously transform us into righteous people. Neither will we be magically "saved." He has implanted within us a divine soul that gives us the ability to *choose*. And He demands that we use that capacity to choose the *good*.

Therefore we must soberly recognize that there is a lot of work that needs to be done. We must assiduously pursue truth and strive to live by it in *all* areas of life. We must not be deterred by failures and setbacks. We must never quit the moral and spiritual battlefield. Bamidbar is a Book that gives us hope, but does not relieve us of responsibility.

We should remember that in spite of the many tragedies recounted in Bamidbar, the Jewish People *did* enter the Promised Land and established a society which rose to great heights. Both Temples were destroyed and a long and bitter Exile ensued. And yet, our generation has been granted the privilege to witness and participate in the fulfillment of the great Biblical prophecy of the return and regeneration of National Jewish existence.

This historical odyssey has been a long and difficult one, but Bamidbar inspires us to believe that the vision of mankind perfected and redeemed and a world at peace and harmony *will* be achieved. May it happen speedily and in our time.

BAMIDBAR

Significance of a Census

You Were There

Were We Coerced?

Torah is Freedom

Significance of a Census

Parshat Bamidbar initiates the fourth Book of the Torah. It begins with God's command to take a census of the people, according to their tribes.

The concept of a tribe has great importance in Judaism. The nation, at that time, was comprised differentiated groups, each with its own skills and special talents. The challenge was to work together harmoniously for the greater good of the *klal* (community).

The idea of a headcount seems, at first glance, mundane. The Torah is not a work of history and does not record every detail in the life of the nation.

While it may have been important to establish the number of Jews living at that time, why must the Torah devote so much space to the method? What is the spiritual significance of the description of how Moses tallied the Jews?

Significance of a Census

Rashi explains that the census has great importance as an expression of God's love for His people, saying that He counts them "at all times" (Rashi on Bamidbar 1:1). He did so when the Jews left Egypt to embark on the great journey to become a "treasured" nation. He also counts them in times of tragedy, such as after the sin of the Golden Calf, to determine how many survived.

This parsha takes place in the second month (Iyar) of the second year after leaving Egypt. The *Mishkan* had been erected the previous month (Nisan), and Hashem was about to cause His Presence to "dwell" there, so another counting was in order. But in order to understand the relationship between these two events, we must comprehend more clearly why a census is an expression of Hashem's love for His people.

Of course, Hashem does not need to make a count to know how many Jews there are. *All* is known to Him. It is, however, *human* nature to count things that are very important to us. For example, we keep track of our financial portfolio because our economic position is a matter of constant preoccupation.

Counting also implies involvement with and supervision of things that matter. A shepherd numbers his sheep because each one is important and requires care. He must always be ready to make the adjustments necessary for the well-being of his flock.

This insight into the nature of counting helps us understand Rashi's assertion that the census is an expression of Hashem's love for His people. The count is purely for our benefit. It demonstrates to us that we are not an ordinary nation, but one that was fashioned by the Creator to serve His purposes.

17

Bamidbar

It is essential for us, at all times and places, to remember who we are and be cognizant of our special national mission. In addition, we must never lose sight of the fact that our unique relationship with Hashem is unbreakable and permanent. He counts us after a grave sin such as the Golden Calf to show that, even at our lowest moment, He is still our God and we are still His People.

Counting also implies the idea of Providential protection. Hashem's great miracles are not things of the past, but are ongoing, if we hearken to His commandments.

This enables us to better understand why Bamidbar is always read close to the holiday of Shavuot. By accepting the Torah, the Jews became a unique nation charged with the mission to be a "Kingdom of Priests and a Holy Nation" (Exodus 19:6). This is the purpose of our national existence and the means by which we merit Hashem's special Providence. May we be successful in that endeavor.

You Were There

Parshat Bamidbar initiates the fourth Book of the Torah, which goes by that name. At its outset, there is a sense of anticipation as the Jews prepare for the final stage of the Exodus: entry into and conquest of the Land that God promised to our Fathers.

However, it doesn't take long for things to unravel. Problems develop, and the final straw that fatefully impacts the history of the Jewish people occurs with the calamity of the spies. It is disappointing that the generation who experienced the great miracles accompanying the Exodus did not merit to inherit *Eretz Yisrael* (the Land of Israel).

Parshat Bamidbar is always read prior to the Festival of Shavuot, known in English as The Festival of Weeks, which we celebrate seven weeks after Passover.

Each of the major holidays have specific *mitzvot* attached to them. On Passover, we are commanded to renounce *chametz* (leavening) and to eat only matzah. The basic obligation is to reenact the story of enslavement to Pharaoh and our miraculous liberation. Sukkot (Tabernacles), which we celebrate in the fall, commemorates the Divine Providence that accompanied the Jews on their trek through the wilderness. As the Torah says, "In Sukkahs (huts) you shall dwell for seven days, in order that your generations shall know that I *housed* the children of Israel in Sukkahs when I took them out of the land of Egypt" (Leviticus 23:42-42). Thus, each holiday has a specific theme, and the *mitzvot* we perform give expression to its central idea.

Shavuot, however, is different. It does not contain any *mitzvah* that represents the purpose of the holiday. So what is the objective of this celebration? More specifically, what is it that we should seek to accomplish on this day?

Shavuot is not a completely *independent* Festival. Its date is determined by a 49-day count that begins on the second night of Passover.

The purpose of the Exodus was to liberate the Jews from bondage. However, this was not fully achieved until the Jews stood on Mount Sinai and uttered the words that changed the course of history: "We will do and we will listen" (Exodus 24:7). It is only through adherence to Torah, its wisdom and code of behavior, that man achieves genuine *human freedom*. In that sense, Shavuot is the culmination of the liberation process begun on Pesach.

However, while the events underlying Passover and Sukkot required the Jews to perform some activity, that is not the case for Shavuot. During the great Revelation, the Jews were passive. No action was demanded of them. They were to *listen and accept*. Only by agreeing to preserve and study the

Torah did the Jews enter the Covenant and become Hashem's *Chosen Nation*.

Thus, there is no specific *mitzvah* connected to Shavuot. However, the holiday is defined in our prayers as "the time of the giving of our Torah."

The key word in that phrase is *our*. The Creator of the universe *gave* the Torah to the Jewish people, and its proper observance forms the entire objective of our national existence. Those of us who were born Jewish cannot be designated as "Jews by choice." The Jews who stood on Mount Sinai accepted the Torah for themselves and for all future generations.

I believe that it is vitally important for each and every Jew to experience his *own* personal *Matan Torah* (giving of the Torah). Therefore, our mission on Shavuot is *not* to perform any particular *mitzvah*, but rather to contemplate the full significance of the great Revelation and to adopt the Torah as our guide to life. Only in this way can we truly render the holiday as "the time of the giving of *our* Torah."

Reading Bamidbar before Shavuot reminds us that the generation that left Egypt, despite all the *wonders* they experienced, did not merit to enter *Eretz Yisrael*. Miracles, however great, are not sufficient to create lasting spiritual transformation. Only the absolute and wholehearted acceptance of Torah, and the determination to *live by it*, can enable the Jews to become a "Kingdom of Priests and a Holy Nation" (Exodus 19:6). May we merit to achieve it.

Were We Coerced?

The Parsha of Bamidbar is always read aloud in Synagogue the week before the holiday of Shavuot, also known as the Festival of Weeks. This festival celebrates the giving of the Torah to the Jewish people on Mount Sinai. This essay, as well as the following one, which both discuss ideas related to Shavuot, are included in the section of Parshat Bamidbar due to its proximity to the holiday.

An Aggadic teaching of the Talmud asserts that the Jews only accepted the Torah because they were coerced.

This idea derives from the verse in Exodus describing the Revelation: "They stood at the base of the mountain" (Exodus 19:17). Rav Avdimi said it teaches that God turned the mountain over them like a vat and told them, "If you accept the Torah, fine, but if not, this will be your burial place" (Talmud Shabbos 88a).

This explanation lends itself to many questions. First and foremost, why would God do this, and what is the benefit of an agreement secured through the fear of destruction?

Another Midrash says that God offered the Torah to various nations, but each rejected it because of its prohibitions

(Sifrei on Devarim 343). Well, why didn't Hashem use the pressure of dire consequences to secure *their* agreement? That selfsame Midrash praises the Jews for their positive reaction to Hashem's offer, but if they assented due to threats, what makes them superior?

Even more problematically, the Aggadic teaching from the Talmud cited above contradicts the plain sense of the scriptural account of the "negotiations" that preceded the Revelation at Sinai, with Moses acting as mediator.

At Hashem's instruction, Moses conveyed God's message, the essence of which was "and now, if you earnestly hearken to my voice and observe my covenant, you will be my most treasured nation, for the entire Earth is Mine" (Exodus 19:5). Upon hearing this "invitation," the "entire people responded as one, and said, 'Everything Hashem spoke, we will do'" (Exodus 19:8). Moses reported this response to God, who proceeded to reveal the *Aseret HaDibrot* (10 Commandments) on Mount Sinai.

There is no hint of threat or coercion in God's communication with the Jews. Hashem stressed the great benefit that would ensue from commitment to the covenant. The Jews would, by accepting the Torah, become a holy nation and God's special treasure.

This seems to be an offer one couldn't refuse. And it doesn't appear that there was any dissent among the people. They were all united in their enthusiastic positive response. That is why the Jews are favorably contrasted with the other nations that could only find fault with the Torah's restrictions and rejected it.

The Rabbi who formulated the Aggada about the mountain turned over them certainly knew the scriptural account. How could he maintain that the people complied only out of fear of death?

There is no doubt in my mind that the Aggada is not meant to be taken literally, but, rather, to convey a subtle message. Humans are complex beings with many levels of thought and intention. We are also capable of ambivalence. Sometimes we are caught in a dilemma when our mind tells us one thing, but our emotions are completely out of sync with what we "know" to be true.

The Jews' positive attitude is described in the Torah and must be taken at the literal level. Hashem's summons to become His special nation resonated with the people. It was very appealing, and they freely accepted it. On the conscious level, they agreed to receive the Torah willingly, happily.

However, the Aggada is pointing out that their emotions were not entirely in line with their conscious attitude. There was psychological resistance to being "locked in" to the system of *mitzvot*. These contrary feelings were so strong that, to stifle them, an element of compulsion was required. The Jews had witnessed the awesome power of God. The fear and reverence in which they held Hashem was a necessary factor in making the decision to become His people.

As we contemplate and prepare ourselves for the anniversary of the Revelation at Sinai, let us review the very nature of our commitment to Judaism. Specifically, do we observe the Torah out of habit and without any particular passion?

Perhaps we are very serious about our religious responsibilities but do we serve Hashem only out of fear. There is nothing wrong with that and, indeed, it would be a wonderful world if all its inhabitants behaved righteously, even if only because of insecurity and trepidation.

However, the Torah maintains that that is not the highest level of religious performance. It urges us to be like "servants who serve their master *not* for the sake of receiving benefits," while still keeping the "fear of Heaven" upon us (Ethics of Our Fathers 1:3). A certain degree of fear is absolutely necessary, but we should aim for the elevated level of *love*.

The "Service of Love" does not come instantaneously or easily. It requires great effort and determination over a long period of time. When a person obtains religious maturity, he recognizes the *objective* beauty of the Torah and its great value in facilitating individual perfection and societal harmony.

As he increases his understanding of the Commandments, he marvels at their great depth and the exquisite understanding of the human condition that they reflect. He is drawn to, and experiences great awe for, the "Statutes of Hashem which are *true*, rejoicing the heart" and the "Commandments of Hashem which are clear, enlightening the eyes" (Psalms 19:9).

We need to recognize that our Torah comes from the Creator of the Universe. Just as the authentic scientist is enraptured by the infinite knowledge which is manifested in the natural order, so too is the genuine Torah scholar captivated by the endless wisdom of Torah. Neither the scientist nor the Torah scholar is motivated by fear of consequences. For when love enters the soul, one runs to serve his Creator with great desire.

May this be the goal of our service of Hashem.

Torah Is Freedom

As mentioned in the introduction to the previous essay, the Parsha of Bamidbar is always read aloud in Synagogue the week before the holiday of Shavuot, also known as the Festival of Weeks. This festival celebrates the giving of the Torah to the Jewish people on Mount Sinai. This essay, as well as the preceding one, which both discuss ideas related to Shavuot, are included in the section of Parshat Bamidbar due to its proximity to the holiday.

In the week that follows the reading of Parshat Bamidbar in synagogue, we celebrate the *chag* (holiday) of Shavuot, which means "weeks" -- a strange name for a unique day. The titles of other special occasions reflect their basic theme, such as Passover, Yom Kippur, and Rosh Hashanah. Whence does Shavuot derive its unusual designation?

While it falls on the 6th of Sivan, that date is not listed in the Torah. The dates of the other holidays are explicitly mentioned in the Torah as, for example, regarding Pesach; it says, "On the fifteenth of this month (Nisan), there shall be a festival of Matzot unto Hashem..." (Leviticus 23:6). The same is true for the other holy days.

Shavuot is not assigned a special date. Rather, we are instructed to count seven weeks and proclaim the next day as the holiday of Shavuot. Inevitably, this will fall on the 6th of Sivan. Its holiness does not, however, derive from anything unique about that particular date, but only because it is the day that follows the seven-week count.

What is the reason for this seeming anomaly?

Shavuot is not an entirely independent institution. Rather, it must be seen as the culmination of the festival of Passover.

When Hashem instructed Moses to go to Pharaoh, He told him, "This is the sign that I have sent you, when you take the nation out of Egypt, they will worship Me on this mountain" (Exodus 3:12).

The Exodus was not an end in itself, but the means for the Jews to experience the Revelation at Mount Sinai and become Hashem's special nation. Thus, the holidays of Pesach and Shavuot form one unit. The bridge that connects them is the seven-week count.

Why isn't Pesach a stand-alone phenomenon? Aren't the events we recount at the Seder so monumental that they warrant a celebration of their own, without association with another significant happening?

The answer resides in the unique Jewish concept of freedom. The Rabbis say that, at Sinai, Hashem hung the mountain over them and declared that "If you accept the Torah, it will be good but if you reject it, this will be your burial place" (Talmud Shabbos 88a).

Bamidbar

We cannot take literally the implication that the Jews received the Torah not voluntarily, but only out of coercion. That would contradict the plain sense of the verse, which tells that, in response to Hashem's offer, "the entire nation responded as one and said 'everything that Hashem says, we will do'" (Exodus 19:8).

The Rabbis do not mean that Hashem pressured the Jews with death threats to keep His commandments. Such religious observance would have no spiritual value, as it would not emanate from man's free will.

What the Rabbis mean to convey is that, on a certain psychological level, the Jews had "no choice." Put yourself in their position. They had witnessed, at first hand, Hashem's awesome power, most significantly in His utter destruction of the Egyptian army at the *Yam Suf* (Sea of Reeds). How could anyone entertain the thought of refusing His offer to give them His Torah? Out of a profound sense of awe at the might of Hashem, the Jews said *yes* to the Torah.

So why did the Rabbis use language that implies coercion? What is the meaning of the threat that, if they refuse, "This will be your burial place"?

The words didn't mean that Hashem would slay them for refusing. After all, He has given us free will and allows us to chart our own course. As the Rabbis comment, "To the place a person seeks to go, there we bring him" (Talmud Makkot 10b). Moreover, tradition also teaches that Hashem offered the Torah to all the nations, and they refused it. There is no indication that *these* recalcitrants were destroyed.

In my opinion, the words "your burial place" are not intended literally. Instead, they mean that, if you accept the Torah, you will achieve the true purpose of life, but if you do not, you will be "as good as dead." A life without the enlightenment of Torah and the pleasantness of its lifestyle and ideals is *not worth living*.

Consequently, Passover, which celebrates the physical liberation from Egypt, cannot be a holiday by itself. The enslavement was evil because it prevented the Jews from exercising their minds and pursuing a life of understanding and moral perfection. Hashem extricated us from the servitude to Pharaoh only so we could become *His* servants.

We count the days from the Exodus to the Revelation at Sinai, because this is the season to reflect on the purpose of life and the true meaning of freedom. It is the time when we seek to break the bonds of our numerous enslavements and embrace the service of Hashem, which embodies true freedom.

That is why the anniversary of *Maamad Har Sinai* (Revelation at Mount Sinai) is known as the Holiday of Weeks. This indicates that this special day is the culmination of a process that began with the Exodus from Egypt but concluded with *Matan Torah*. The Torah is thereby communicating its special concept of human freedom.

Contrary to contemporary thinking, the absence of practical restraints and the enjoyment of unlimited political rights does not add up to genuine freedom. For man can very easily slide into a state of moral subservience to false ideals and empty fantasies.

Only the person who is rooted in study of true ideas and energetic practice of righteous behavior liberates himself from a life of falsehood and irrational goals.

Of course we celebrate the obtainment of practical liberty which was achieved with the Exodus. However, the holiday of *Weeks* teaches us that human autonomy is not an end in itself but only the necessary condition enabling us to

Bamidbar

pursue the liberation of the soul contained in the ideas and way of life prescribed in the Torah. May we merit to achieve it.

NASO

The Vindicated Adulteress

Reverence for the Soul

Sins of the Scholars

Spiritual Dining

The Vindicated Adulteress

Parshat Naso contains the law of the *sotah*, or "strayed woman." This refers to a Jewish wife who has played "fast and loose" with her marital restrictions. Married Jews must avoid flirtatious interactions with members of the opposite sex. What happens when a married woman gets too cozy with a strange man and the husband fears that matters are hurtling out of control? He has the power to issue a *warning* that she avoid being secluded with the suspected paramour, the violation of which can have lethal consequences.

Judaism takes the institution of marriage very seriously, in contradistinction to contemporary culture. Our current lax attitude has led to a divorce rate of over 50%, and this has wreaked havoc on the sustainability of the family unit. Yet the basis of a stable and moral society is a family unit built upon functional and enduring marriages.

Unlike other religions, however, Judaism does not prohibit divorce, because it acknowledges the weaknesses of human nature. It realizes that there will always be people who, with the best of intentions, will err in their selection of a mate. Or perhaps the choice was right at the moment but could not withstand the "test of time." It is only natural that, in the course of things, people evolve emotionally and philosophically until the bonds that once united them are torn asunder.

We should not take the decision to "split" lightly. When one experiences problems in his marriage, he should not rush to judgment. People's natural tendency is to put the blame on their partners. A mature person should realize that "it takes two to tango" and be able to look within and affirm how his *own* flaws have contributed to the problem.

When a marriage falters, one should seek help and strive to remedy the problems.

Judaism recognizes, however, that this is not always possible. One of the parties may be at the point where the situation is unbearable, and they "can't take it anymore." In these cases, our religion allows the dissolution of the union. No one is obligated to be trapped in a miserable relationship that negates their basic right to happiness.

However, we must be very diligent in maintaining the viability of marriages.

The case of the *sotah* illustrates how strict the Torah is regarding spousal behavior. It looks askance upon a married person engaging in inappropriate and suggestive behaviors with strangers. Many laws were established to prevent people from entering into situations which, while seemingly innocent, can lead to sin.

The *sotah* has strayed because she has been secluded with another man, and this has aroused her husband's jealousy.

Naso

He fears that she may be on the brink of an extramarital affair and wants to prevent that in order to preserve his marriage.

The Torah provides him with a *halachic* mechanism to address the situation, wherein he *warns* his wife, in the presence of two witnesses, not to be alone with that man. She may still communicate with the gentleman, but may not be with him in a setting that is conducive to romantic temptations.

If the woman then defies her husband's warning and is found to have met privately with the forbidden male, she has placed the marriage in jeopardy. In a case of actual adultery, the husband *must* divorce her. But, in this instance, we are in doubt: we don't have evidence of an actual tryst, but the situation is extremely suspicious.

Until this matter is resolved, the couple must cease living together as man and wife. The husband may divorce her if he chooses. However, the woman can protest her innocence of a physical relationship and demand to be tested by the "bitter waters" of the *sotah*.

This unique procedure is founded upon a miracle in which God intervenes to mete out justice to the suspects. A scroll is prepared containing a curse which states that if she sinned, she will experience a horrible and unnatural death. This Parchment, which contains the name of Hashem, is placed in water and thereby erased. The woman drinks the water which, in effect, tests her. If she is truly innocent, nothing will happen to her and her reputation will be restored. But, if adultery has been committed, she and her lover (wherever he happens to be at that moment) will experience a horrible death.

It is interesting to note that the Rabbis do all in their power to convince her not to undergo this ordeal. However, if she adamantly insists on doing so, she can't be stopped.

The Vindicated Adulteress

Ordinarily, it is a grave sin to erase the Divine name. Yet in the case of the *sotah* this is permitted in order to demonstrate the extreme importance of a harmonious marital relationship. Hashem, as it were, allows His Holy Name to be erased in order to demonstrate the supreme significance of *Shalom Bayit* (family tranquility).

The *sotah* who is found to be innocent will resume the marital relationship with her husband. Not only that, but she will be rewarded by Hashem with healthy and beautiful children.

We cannot avoid asking this challenging question: why does she deserve a reward? True, she is innocent of adultery, but she did engage in reckless behavior, leading to the test of the waters that prompted the erasure of Hashem's name.

In my opinion, she is rewarded because, at the last moment, she recognized the supreme importance of her marriage, realized the foolishness of her behavior, and refrained from adultery. She was determined to endure the shame and degradation of the *sotah* test to reestablish her shattered union and make it flourish. For this, Hashem rewards her with the greatest gift and most sublime fruit of marriage: wonderful children.

The vindicated *sotah* manifests a certain greatness of spirit. We are all guilty, at some time, of foolish and immature behavior that can wreck our most cherished relationships. Sometimes we just face the consequences and move on.

Or, we can experience a moment in which, against all odds, we return to our senses. Even as we are rushing headlong toward disaster, we can heed the desperate voice within us that cries out to us not to let go of something precious.

There is an important lesson here. It is that even when we are caught up in sin, we should not despair and believe that

Naso

all is lost. We have within us the power to reverse course and embark on a new path based on honesty and courage. If we renounce our sinful tendencies and reach out to Hashem to help us clear our name, He will surely be there to carry us out of the pit. And He will generously reward us.

Reverence for the Soul

Parshat Naso contains the laws that pertain to the institution of *nezirut* (laws pertaining to a Nazir). The Nazir is someone who has taken a vow of *abstention*. The time period for this abstention must be, at the minimum, 30 days. However, it can be for as long as the Nazir specifies in his or her vow.

The main object from which a Nazir must refrain is wine, or even any component of the grape. Additionally, he cannot cut his hair, but must let it grow out. At the conclusion of the Nazirite period, he must bring certain sacrifices and shave off his hair completely.

He is also precluded from defiling himself by coming in contact with a corpse. This applies even to the close relatives for whom one is obligated to mourn, including one's spouse, parents, siblings, and children.

Naso

In this respect the Nazir's status is like that of the *Kohen Gadol* (High Priest).

The only exception to this restriction, for both the *Kohen Gadol* and the Nazir, is the corpse which is referred to as the *meit mitzvah*. Translated literally, this means the *deceased regarding whom there is a mitzvah.*

What circumstances render someone a *meit mitzvah?*

The *halacha* (Jewish law) is that the seven close relatives who are obligated to mourn for a deceased individual are *also* responsible for arranging a proper burial. Since most people pass away leaving some survivors, they are not left in a situation of *need* regarding their interment. However, sometimes a person enjoys a very long life in which he outlives all his next of kin. When *he* dies, there is no mourner who is obligated to arrange his funeral. He thus becomes a *meit mitzvah*.

The phenomenon of a *meit mitzvah* can also occur in a different way. The Rabbis teach that "one who converts is like a newborn baby" (Talmud Yevamos 62a). They mean to say that all of his former familial relationships are *dissolved*. He is, thus, at the outset, a Jew with no relatives. He can, however, *obtain* them by getting married and having children. His spouse and offspring would then, upon his death, be required to bury and mourn for him.

However, should the convert fail to get married and procreate, he would die without next of kin and become a *meit mitzvah*. The rule in this case is that the first Jew to chance upon his body would have to see to his proper burial-- even if that person is the *Kohen Gadol* or a Nazir.

The laws regarding the *meit mitzvah* contain a great teaching about Judaic values and philosophy. All Jews are bound by the commandment, "Thou shalt be Holy" (Leviticus 19:2). The Torah recognizes that there are different degrees of personal *sanctity*. The highest is that of the *Kohen Gadol* and the Nazir.

The High Priest is the only one who can enter the "Holy of Holies" in the Temple and perform the special service that secures forgiveness for the Jewish people on Yom Kippur, the Day of Atonement. He cannot come in contact with his deceased close relatives, because the verse states, "And from the Sanctuary he may not depart" (Leviticus 21:12), which the Rabbis interpret to mean that he may not abandon his state of holiness.

The same concept applies to the Nazir. The verse states, "All the days of his *nezirut* he is holy unto Hashem" (Numbers 6:8).

We shouldn't think, from the case of the Nazir, that a person obtains an elevated stature simply abstaining from pleasure. It is not a *mitzvah* to deprive oneself of any enjoyment that this world offers. The Rambam states that living an ascetic existence is prohibited and that this is the religious approach of idolaters (Mishneh Torah, Hichot Deot 3:1).

However, he warns, we are not to embrace extreme indulgence and become wholly absorbed in carnal gratifications. Rather, we should seek the "middle way," satisfying our needs in a controlled and intelligent manner to maintain health in body and soul.

Therefore, under ordinary circumstances, Judaism does *not* believe that a person should renounce enjoyment of wine.

To the contrary, the verse states that "wine rejoices the heart of man" (Psalms 104:15). Because of this, we recite *Kiddush* over wine on Shabbat and drink it on the *chagim* (holidays) when we are commanded to "rejoice in your Festivals" (Deuteronomy 16:14).

Naso

The Nazir renounces wine for a prescribed period of time because he has decided to embark on a profound spiritual transformation. He is abandoning a lifestyle based on the pursuit of pleasure and transitioning into one based on the elevation of the soul through wisdom and good deeds. He is putting all his energy into intense introspection, study, and closeness to the Creator.

When man discovers his Creator and devotes all of his energy to living according to His Will, he attains the *highest* state of *kedusha* (holiness). He is, indeed, on a par with the *Kohen Gadol*, and neither may defile themselves by contact with a corpse, regardless of the closeness of the relationship.

Except for the *meit mitzvah*, who might very well be on the lowest rung of the social ladder.

This exception occurs because Judaism attaches great significance to the concern for *human dignity*, especially in the matter of a respectful burial. The dignity of man is a value that Judaism taught the world, and the doctrine of human rights is founded upon it, based on the verse in Genesis which states, "And God created man in His Image, in the Image of God created He him, male and female created He them" (Genesis 1:27). We honor the divine soul by respecting the dead and, by extension, the One who implanted it in the human body.

This is a vital lesson regarding the Jewish concept of holiness. Even when a person is immersed in his personal desire to reach a higher level in his relationship with Hashem, he can't close his eyes to the world around him.

He must still be concerned about his fellow man. He must surrender his state of ritual purity to perform what the Rabbis refer to as the *chesed shel emet* (compassion of truth).

A Nazir must get personally involved in the details of interring a total stranger, even one who does not occupy a significant place in society. The *Kohen Gadol* must disqualify himself from performing the holiest and most vital Service in the Temple to prevent any disrespect to the soul of a fellow Jew whose only need is for a proper burial.

If we are commanded to be so solicitous to the requirements of a corpse that experiences no pain or shame, how much more so should we be sensitive to and generous with the wants of a living being whom we have chanced upon and who needs our help. Recognizing the dignity of man because he is imbued with the divine soul is the most exalted form of honoring Hashem. May we merit to attain it.

Sins of the Scholars

The Parsha of Naso describes the special manner in which the Tabernacle was inaugurated. The procedure took place over the course of twelve days, in which every prince was assigned a separate day to bring special sacrifices on behalf of himself and the tribe that he led.

It is significant that the investiture of the *Mishkan* was accomplished by the leaders of the People acting on behalf of those they represented. In doing so, a bond was forged between the tribal units that were the constituent elements of the Nation.

Cooperation between the Tribes and the national government was absolutely essential for the wellbeing of the Jewish People. This required the elimination of strife and fostering of a spirit of love among all Jews.

Sadly, the ideal of brotherly love has not always been prevalent among the Jews. Our history is marked by its fair share of internal strife and conflict. In fact, the Temple was destroyed because of the sin of "baseless hatred."

The time period between the holidays of Passover and Shavuot, which is generally referred to as the Omer, contains profound illustrations of this idea. There are two distinct religious practices in effect at this time. Starting from the second night of Passover, we initiate a count of the 49 days which constitutes the 7 weeks that bring us to the holiday of Shavuot.

In the days of the Temple, when sacrifices were brought, this count was a Biblical commandment. According to most commentators, it is, in the absence of the Temple, no longer a Torah requirement.

Nevertheless, the Rabbis mandated that we do this count as a remembrance of the Sanctuary. That is why, after enumerating the pertinent day, we utter this short but meaningful prayer: "May the Merciful One restore the Temple service to its place, speedily in our days, Amen."

Many customs have been established to ensure that we will remember the destruction of the Temple. This does not simply mean that we should recall it as an historical occurrence. Every Jew is aware that we once had the Holy Temple and, due to our sins, no longer have it. There is no danger that this piece of information will be lost.

Rather, the point is that we should be cognizant of the enormous spiritual loss we have endured and cultivate a yearning for a return to *Eretz Yisrael* and the rebuilding of the Temple.

Thus, we put ashes above the forehead of the groom under the *chuppah* (marriage canopy), and he smashes a glass at the conclusion of the marriage ceremony. This act is accompanied by the recitation of the relevant verse from

Naso

Psalms that implores us to place the remembrance of Jerusalem above our most significant joy: "If I forget you, O Jerusalem, let my right hand wither; let my tongue stick to my palate if I cease to think of you, if I do not keep Jerusalem in memory even at my happiest hour" (Psalms 137:5-6).

In my opinion, these practices imply that a Jew should always retain a sense of discomfiture with the fact that he is in Exile. Admittedly, this is not easy in America, where, from every material and political vantage point, we "have it made." To long for the restoration of Zion in our current condition requires a great sensitivity to the spiritual beauty that we miss in our separation from *Yerushalayim* (Jerusalem).

There is an additional feature that marks the time of the Omer: the custom to observe a period of mourning for 33 days.

According to our classical sources, a terrible plague, which took the lives of 24,000 students of Rabbi Akiva, one of the greatest Sages in history, took place during the Omer. The Rabbis explain that this was not an ordinary disaster brought about by purely natural causes. Rather, this calamity was a manifestation of Divine punishment. These great Torah scholars were afflicted because they failed to display the proper respect to one another.

At first glance, this is difficult to comprehend. How is it possible that the choicest scholars who had the privilege of learning under one of the greatest teachers could lack so elemental a virtue as *derech eretz* (decent manners)? The study of Torah is the most spiritual activity anyone can be involved in.

It can, however, be a double-edged sword. It can purify the personality and create a sense of humility and a sublime appreciation for the supreme wisdom of the Giver of the

Torah. Conversely, nothing arouses man's ego more than the attainment of knowledge.

Jewish life is dominated by great respect for the *talmid chacham* (Torah scholar). We put our Sages on a pedestal and look up to them with the greatest reverence. Thus, some may be attracted to Torah study precisely because they crave the honor that goes with it. The pursuit of recognition and prestige can lead to disrespect and disdain for one's fellow students and colleagues.

We learn from this that the goal of Torah study is not just the attainment of knowledge, but the refinement of the personality and perfection of the soul.

We must also deduce from this calamity that Torah scholars are held to higher standards and judged more severely than "ordinary" people. While it is wrong for anyone to be disrespectful, when that behavior is committed by someone who is not a Torah scholar, he will not necessarily meet with such harsh punishment.

Rabbi Soloveitchik asked that, since we must assume these scholars did *teshuva* (repentance), why wasn't that sufficient to annul the evil decree? He answered by citing the Rambam, who says that repentance attains forgiveness for all sins, with one exception. When a person desecrates the name of God in the course of his transgression, he does not receive pardon until death, and thus must bear the consequences of the sin in this world (Mishneh Torah Hilchos Teshuva 1:4).

Disrespect would not be a capital offense for an ordinary person, but, when committed by a Torah scholar, it desecrates the name of Hashem and His Torah.

It is appropriate that the national mourning take place during the time we perform the *mitzvah* of Counting the Omer. We do so to remember the tragic destruction of the Holy

Naso

Temple, a major cause of which was baseless hatred. The seriousness of this sin is illustrated by the tragedy of Rabbi Akiva's students.

Parshat Naso depicts the manner in which the Temple was dedicated. All of the leaders participated by bring special offerings to Hashem. This demonstrated their great desire to serve the serve the nation and strengthen it through forging solid bonds of unity.

It is vitally important that spiritual leaders, especially Torah scholars and their students, eschew ego and the desire for renown. Doing so will bring great honor to the Jewish Nation and that is the glory we should pursue.

Spiritual Dining

The Parsha of Naso introduces us to a unique individual known as a Nazir. This man or woman has been moved to take a vow of abstention from wine and every component of the grape. In addition, the Nazir cannot shave the hair on his head, nor is he permitted to come in contact with a corpse.

Regarding this matter, his status is the same as that of the *Kohen Gadol*, who may not contract ritual impurity even for his closest blood relatives. The clear implication is that the Torah places great value upon the renunciation of bodily pleasures.

This inference, however, flies in the face of many Rabbinical statements that take a very harsh attitude towards the negation of fundamental biological and psychological necessities. Judaism, unlike most religions, does not extol the practice of extremism. In his many writings, the Rambam

Naso

states unequivocally that the governing principle of Jewish moral behavior is *moderation*. In virtually every area of instinctual activity, we are to seek out "the golden mean," the place that is equidistant from both extremes.

Thus, we are supposed to exercise discipline and control in the gratification of our desires. For example, when we eat, we must first and foremost recognize that activity's purpose. The function of food is to provide the nourishment we need to maintain good health.

It is also true that eating certain types of food can be very pleasurable. The culinary experience is a multibillion-dollar enterprise. Is there anything wrong with indulging oneself with the dishes one finds most appealing?

The answer to that question is not simple. How should a person blend the health factor with the element of pleasure? Must one choose between eating exclusively for health and eating for enjoyment?

The philosophy of moderation can resolve the conflict. One must first recognize that everything Hashem created has a purpose. Clearly, the first consideration in deciding one's eating habits should be healthiness. However, we must also recognize that God implanted in us the faculty of taste, which when gratified, provides enormous satisfaction.

Therefore, we should choose a diet based on the principle of health. However, this still allows us to partake of many different foods, which we can prepare in the tastiest manner. Thus it is possible to gratify the true biological purpose of eating and also to partake of its pleasure.

The problem arises when there is a conflict between these two factors. Sometimes a person has a medical condition that severely restricts his food choices. In fact, often the foods a person craves the most are harmful to him. The philosophy of moderation demands that a person must put aside the pleasure component and embrace that of health. He must eat a wholesome diet, even if it means he has to sacrifice the joys of the palate.

The concept of moderation applies to every area of life. One should not think that holiness consists of going to the extremes of abstinence and self-denial. A person who afflicts his body with fasting and deprivation is, according to the Rambam, a fool and a sinner. We should not seek to be something that we are not. We must serve God as human beings, not angels.

He created us with many needs, and we must satisfy them, intelligently and properly, to keep ourselves in the best possible shape for leading a constructive life. That is why it is so important to care for our health, both physical and mental. Pain of the body or mind seriously impedes spiritual growth and renders the goal of serving Hashem difficult to attain.

There are, however, two cases where one must go to extremes. One may *not* express anger in moderation, but must go to the extreme of uprooting it from his psyche. Similarly with ego. One should renounce it completely and seek to be as humble as possible.

Ego and anger destroy the soul and "remove" a person from this world. A calm and modest spirit is essential to enjoying this life and displaying gratitude to the One Who made it possible.

It should be noted that man by nature is attracted and drawn to *extreme* forms of behavior. The philosophy of moderation is unglamorous and not emotionally exciting. However, the wise person who wants to live in accordance with the lifestyle mandated by the Torah will embrace the healing and fulfilling approach of the "Golden Mean."

BEHA'ALOTCHA

The True Leader

Was Jethro Selfish?

Jews By Choice

Judaism Must Inspire Unity and Love

Rebellion in the Wilderness

The True Leader

The book of Bamidbar contains more tragedies than any other in the Torah.

This is not to say that other calamities had not occurred. In *Shemot* (Exodus), we read about the Golden Calf, which brought the people to the brink of annihilation. Fortunately, Moses had stood in the breach and found the right prayer to assuage God's wrath. The situation improved as Moses delivered the second set of tablets. The people proceeded to build the *Mishkan*, which was a monumental national achievement. All told, the Jews had spent a year encamped around Mount Sinai, receiving the Torah from Moses and building the Sanctuary.

The next order of business was positioning the tribes around the *Mishkan* for the trek to the Promised Land. All the wilderness tasks had been accomplished, and the nation was ready to proceed to the long-awaited conquest and inheritance of the Land. In a mood of exuberance, Moses enthusiastically invited his father-in-law, Jethro, to join them and partake of the great good that Hashem had promised to His people.

However, no one, even the greatest prophet, can anticipate the future. There was no way Moses could discern what lay in store for him in his mission to bring the people to the chosen land.

In Parshat Beha'alotcha, we encounter a "food rebellion" launched by a segment of the nation. The protesters expressed their dissatisfaction with the *Manna*, the special food Hashem had designed to sustain the Jews in the Wilderness. It was the most perfect nourishment anyone could want: nutritious, tasty, and extremely versatile. It required little exertion on the part of the people. All they had to do was take a stroll every morning and encounter the Divine gift "wrapped" in dew. They would then gather their daily needs and bring it to their tents, where they would prepare it in the manner they desired.

In spite of its great qualities, the people found fault with the *Manna*. Suddenly, they remembered the "wonderful" foods they had enjoyed in Egypt, free. Now they had nothing to look forward to, except the *Manna*.

We should not judge anyone until we have been in his place. From our vantage point, it is exceedingly easy and tempting to criticize the people for their unworthy behavior. The point in contemplating it is not to feel superior, but to seek to learn the relevant lessons of this dire episode.

The people's behavior took a severe toll on Moses. Even the sin of the Golden Calf had not shaken his resolve to defend and plead for the people in the most precarious circumstances. Yet, here we encounter an entirely different and unexpected response from the great leader.

Beha'alotcha

Moses expressed his anguish that God had brought evil to him by placing the burden of this nation on him. He complained that there was no way he could supply the endless needs of the Jewish people.

He asked, "Did I conceive this entire people? Did I give birth to them, that You say to me, 'Carry them in your bosom, like the nurse carries the sucking infant, to the land that you swore to his forefathers'?" (Numbers 11:12). Moses then pleaded with Hashem to appoint others to share the burden of leadership with him. If this could not be done, he implored that Hashem should take his life, so he would not witness the harm that would ensue from his inadequate leadership.

Moses' words are truly amazing. Only the most humble of men could express his most intense and visceral thoughts to the Creator of the universe, without it being regarded as base arrogance. What is it about this food rebellion that put Moses in such a state of despair and reluctance to continue as the leader?

A key to understanding this story lies in Moses' metaphor of the nursing mother. What did Moses mean by saying that God had told him to carry the Jewish people in his bosom?

Rabbi Soloveitchik explains that this rebellion was unique. The building of the Golden Calf was motivated by fear and insecurity. Moses did not seek to relinquish his leadership at that time because he believed that, with the proper instruction, he could raise the Jewish people to a higher level. Moses felt that his main function was to educate them about true ideals and thus to elevate them spiritually. In fact, he was willing to spend the entire day answering their questions and resolving their disputes, without any reservations.

However, the rebellion over food was a different phenomenon. It was not based on false ideas, but on the descent into lust. Instead of involving themselves in the life of moderation and discipline represented by the *Manna*, the people demanded that their appetitive cravings be satisfied. They were embracing the hedonistic way of life that views sensual gratification as the highest ideal.

Moses recognized that his role as teacher and intellectual leader would not suffice for the new situation. The people now needed personal attention to guide them in every area of their lives. A new system of multiple leaders and role models was now required, and Moses prayed fervently to Hashem to modify the leadership model.

We thus see that Moses had no desire to abandon the people. Because he was so dedicated to their needs, he was prescient enough to know that major changes were needed. Of course, this meant that he would have to bring others on board and to share power with them. His humility and devotion to the Jewish People only served to make the sharing of power a desirable prospect because it would better serve the People's needs.

May we have the wisdom to recognize and acknowledge the problems in our midst as well as the need for change when necessary, and the humility to put ego aside and to do what is required for the greater good of the God's *Chosen Nation*.

Was Jethro Selfish?

Parshat Beha'alotcha talks about the beginning of the Jewish people's journey to *Eretz Yisrael*.

The Jews had spent an entire year camped around Mount Sinai. During this time, their major occupation was the study of the Torah that Hashem revealed to Moses. They also engaged in the great project of constructing the *Mishkan*.

All of this spiritually prepared them to enter the Land, build the *Beit HaMikdash* (Holy Temple), and transform themselves into a "wise and discerning" nation. The plan was to make a quick journey through the wilderness, followed by invasion and conquest of the Land.

That sequence of events was what Hashem "wanted," but things do not always work out as planned. God conferred free will upon man, which thus enables him to "thwart" the Divine Plan. The generation that had experienced enslavement in Egypt ultimately could not overcome their limitations and succumbed to the fear-mongering of the spies.

The episode of the spies, which delayed the conquest, was to occur later. At this point, Moses believed that the people were embarking on the journey and would be at the gates of the Promised Land in just a matter of days. It is interesting that even the greatest prophet did not know what lay ahead. Hashem alone decides what information to reveal to a prophet, even the most exalted one, to whom God spoke "face to face."

The Torah records an intriguing discussion between Moses and his distinguished father-in-law, Jethro. It would appear that Jethro wanted to return to his homeland of Midian. He had come when he heard about the great miracles that Hashem had wrought when delivering the Jews from Egypt.

Jethro's goal was to learn about the Exodus in depth with the greatest teacher, *Moshe Rabbenu* (Moses Our Teacher). The lessons had a great impact on him, so he brought sacrifices and uttered praises to Hashem. In fact, Jethro converted to Judaism and, according to some, was present at the Revelation. Interestingly, he did not return home at that time. Instead, he spent the entire year with the Jewish encampment around Mount Sinai.

It was only now, when they were breaking camp and embarking on the trek to Israel, that he decided it was time to go. Moses implored him to join the people in their journey to the Land, so he might share in the "goodness" that God had promised them. Surprisingly, Jethro refused, and Moses tried again. He said, "Please do not abandon us, for you know our encampment in the desert, and you have been for us as eyes. And when you come with us, all the goodness that Hashem bestows on us, He will bestow on you" (Numbers 10:31-32).

Beha'alotcha

This dialogue is difficult to understand. Why would Jethro not want to continue his life as a Jew by residing in the Land? If his intention in leaving Midian was merely to spend some time studying with Moses, why did he stay with the Jews for the entire year? Could it be that he was content to dwell with them in the desert, but not to live with them in the Land "which flows with milk and honey"?

Rabbi Soloveitchik gave a unique and fascinating explanation. Jethro had a powerful thirst for knowledge. The year spent at Sinai was one in which the people were completely immersed in studying the Torah, written and oral, that Moses conveyed to them.

However, now the period of intensive and exclusive learning was over. The Jews were embarking on a new venture, the conquest of a land and establishment of a state. Jethro did not want to spend his time engaged in these activities. He wanted to return home, where he had all his necessities, and resume his full-time immersion in the study of Torah.

On the basis of this interpretation, I would like to explain Moses's response to Jethro's initial refusal of his invitation. Moses was imploring him to partake of the "good" that God had in store for them in Israel. I believe he meant that it is very nice to go off and study Torah by yourself in Midian. But if is a greater good to build up the nation and establish its religious infrastructure in the land Hashem has designated for the Jews.

One must study Torah for himself, of course, but needs to consider others as well. There was nothing wrong with Jethro's desire to perfect himself by studying Torah with the master teacher, *Moshe Rabbenu*. Selfishness which is rooted in pursuit of the true spiritual purpose of life is a great virtue.

However, one must recognize that the individual benefits only because of a system of instruction that has been set up by Hashem. He taught Moses, who did not keep the knowledge to himself but shared it with all who sought it. When a person taps into that wellspring of wisdom he acquires an obligation to join the community of scholars and make Torah available to others as well.

This is fully in line with his selfish ambitions. That is because there is no more effective form of learning than teaching. Sharing one's ideas with challenging students who are free to analyze and question them enables the teacher to expand his understanding and bring it to a level of profundity otherwise unattainable. He also participates in Hashem's plan to perfect mankind through the educational influence of His chosen nation who are described as an *Or Lagoyim* (light unto the nations) (Isaiah 49:6).

That is why Moses pleaded with his father-in-law not to separate from the nation. He told him that it was fine that he had acquired such significant Torah knowledge, but that it would be a mistake to abandon the source from which he had gained it and return home.

Rather, he said, there is a great good that Hashem has prepared for us in the land of Israel. Jewish national existence is tied in with the Divine plan for the perfection of mankind. Whoever joins the community and contributes to making it source of light for mankind achieves thereby the greatest human fulfillment. May we merit to achieve it.

Jews by Choice

Parshat Beha'alotcha describes the sanctification of the Levites for their service in the *Mishkan*.

Originally this privilege was to be distributed in a more "democratic" fashion. It was not to be confined to one tribe, but available to any *bechor*, that is, the first-born male in a family.

The *bechor* had a special status in the Jewish nation. To this day, the father must "redeem" this child in a ceremony known as *pidyon haben*. This *mitzvah* originated in the last plague that Hashem visited upon Egypt, the slaying of the firstborn.

In executing this judgment, Hashem distinguished between the Jewish males, whom He protected, and the Egyptian offspring, who were destroyed. When we are the beneficiaries of Divine favor, we incur a debt. The *bechor* must recognize that he was saved in order to serve Hashem. It was intended that he would assist the *kohanim* (priests) in their Temple service.

Unfortunately, this great benefit was rescinded because of the sin of the Golden Calf. The firstborns did not refrain from this transgression. Only the tribe of Levi absolutely avoided the temptation of idolatry. Not only that, but they dealt justice to the sinners without concern for any consequences. Their loyalty to the pure and undiluted worship of the Creator, which is the fundamental foundation of Judaism, facilitated their substitution for the firstborns in the Temple Service.

After completing the construction of the *Mishkan* and the consecration of its priests, the people embarked upon the journey that would bring them, in a very short time, to the gates of the Promised Land. The Torah records a conversation in which Moses implores his father-in-law, Jethro, to join them in their conquest and settlement of the land.

For some reason which is not entirely clear, Jethro demurred, saying, "I will not go but, rather, to my land and birthplace will I go" (Numbers 10:30). Moses persisted, reminding him of how helpful his advice and insight had been, and that if he stayed with them, he would partake of the great good that Hashem had guaranteed His People.

What is so important about this conversation that it warranted inclusion in the Torah? What spiritual lesson are we supposed to derive from it?

Jethro was a great man who had the courage to renounce idolatry and to withstand the persecution that he and his family were subjected to, because of his belief in the true God. He left his home and made the arduous wilderness journey to be reunited with Moses after the Exodus.

Beha'alotcha

Jethro's goal was to study the meaning of the events, in depth, with the greatest teacher, *Moshe Rabbeinu*. The lessons he learned had a transformative impact on Jethro. He blessed Hashem for all that He had done for the Jews, and offered sacrifices to Him. According to the Rabbis, he then converted to Judaism.

In light of this, it is difficult to understand Jethro's reluctance to go with the Jews to the land of Israel. An interpretation of offered by Rashi is illuminating. Commenting on Moses's statement "You will be unto us as eyes," Rashi says, "as beloved as the sockets of our eyes, as it says, and you shall love the stranger (convert)" (Rashi on 10:31).

Apparently, Jethro did not know what standing he would have in the Jewish nation. Moses, therefore, revealed a vital principle of the Torah. The convert is not a second-class citizen or inferior in any way.

It is natural in any organized religion for the establishment to feel superior to the "outsider" or newcomer. Jews may not, however, view themselves as being elevated above those who were not "frum (observant) from birth," nor may they look down, in any way, upon the convert. For Hashem, Himself, has bestowed great honor upon the *ger* (convert).

Two commandments enjoin us to love the stranger. Firstly, he is included in the general *mitzvah* of "and you shall love your friend as yourself" (Leviticus 19:18), as the definition of "friend" in this context is any fellow Jew. Secondly, converts are the subject of a special *mitzvah* designed exclusively for them, "And you shall love the *ger*" (Deuteronomy 10:19). The Rambam, in the Mishneh Torah Hilchot Deot 6:4, teaches that Hashem loves the stranger, as it says, "And He loves the *ger*" (Deuteronomy 10:18). This is because the convert has abandoned his family and nation to come under the protection of the *shechina* (Divine Presence).

Moses reassured Jethro that he would have a prominent place among the Jews and that his talents would be fully utilized and appreciated.

There is a lot that we can learn from Moses's dialogue with his father-in-law. Most of us did not choose to be Jewish and often take it for granted. We must look within ourselves and ask; do we harbor innate feelings of superiority? Do we respect the genuine convert with a full heart and recognize his greatness or do we seek to keep him at a certain distance?

Would we be Jewish if we didn't have to, if we had had the choice to be relieved of the "yoke of the commandments"? If fate had dealt us a different hand, would we have the courage and commitment to leave our family and cast our lot with the Jews, simply because of our love for Hashem and His Torah?

Although we will never know, we should be inspired to recognize that such "Jews by choice" do exist and are to be respected and loved. Beyond that they constitute a challenge to our brand of religiosity which is, essentially, a matter of upbringing and social habit.

We should be inspired to emulate the path of the *ger* who discovered the pathway that leads to the love of Hashem and His Service. We should seek out the authentic converts among us to hear their stories and be inspired by them. There is much that they can teach us, for they are true Jewish heroes.

Judaism Must Inspire Unity and Love

Parshat Beha'alotcha begins on a high note, but the upbeat feeling does not endure. It doesn't take very long before we encounter unexpected and disturbing manifestations of rebelliousness. In my opinion, the Book of Bamidbar is essentially *tragic*. At its center is the episode of the *spies*, which brings the Jewish people to the brink of destruction.

However, that catastrophe should not be viewed as an isolated event. It was the result of some deeper problems that were incubating beneath the surface, as this Parsha shows. The generation of the Exodus was supposed to become a Holy Nation by receiving the Torah and entering into a covenant with Hashem. After erecting the *Mishkan*, they were to conquer and settle the Land Hashem promised to Abraham and become there a "Kingdom of Priests and a Holy Nation"

(Exodus 19:6). All of the goals had been attained. Yet the final challenge eluded them.

Sometimes a person is charged with a serious mission comprised of multiple parts. He may be initially successful and discharge all the responsibilities except for the final one. Suddenly and inexplicably, doubts and misgivings emerge, and he is thrown into a paralyzing state of conflict. Will he be able to go *all the way*?

In that sense, Beha'alotcha is a prelude to the story of the spies depicted in the Parsha that follows it, Shelach. Suddenly the people become *mitonenim*, depressed and extremely *discontented*, in a way that was "evil in the sight of Hashem" (Numbers 11:1).

The people's unhappy mood caused them to rebel against their limited diet of *manna* and the absence of manifold culinary delicacies.

It is difficult for us to understand the problem they were having. The Torah openly testifies to *manna*'s wonderful qualities and the ease with which it was gathered. *Manna* was the ideal nutrition in every possible way and should have been the last thing to arouse grumbling. What is going on here?

In this Parsha, Moses tries to convince his father-in-law, Jethro, to join the Jews in their epic journey into the *Promised Land*. Apparently sensing Jethro's reluctance, Moses proclaimed "*We* are journeying to the place concerning which Hashem said, I will give it to you; come with us, and we shall bestow *good* upon you, for Hashem has promised good things for Israel" (Numbers 10:29). What is so important about this dialogue that it warrants inclusion in the Torah?

Rav Soloveitchik famously told his students that whenever he read this verse, he would cry. He then challenged

Beha'alotcha

them: "What is it in this verse that makes me cry?" A number of students tried to guess the answer, but none succeeded.

Finally, he told them that what brings him to tears is that Moses said, "*We* are journeying." At that time Moses fully believed that he was going to lead the Jews into *Eretz Yisrael*, and this filled him with great enthusiasm. He didn't know that this was not to be, that Hashem had other plans for him. And that made the Rav cry.

In my opinion, the Torah records this dialogue to *contrast* Moses's attitude to living in Israel with that of the Jews. This discussion is immediately followed by the stories of the "miserable ones" (*mitonenim*) and the *Manna Rebellion*. This makes it clear that the Jews were in a state of mourning, not great joy, in anticipation of the adventure of becoming an *Am Kadosh* (Holy Nation) in Hashem's Land. They did not share Moses's unbounded enthusiasm; in effect, they did not want to abandon the *Galut* (Exile).

If this is true, why did they accept the Torah and affirm, "We will do and we will listen" (Exodus 24:7)? Wouldn't it automatically follow that they would *desire* to inherit the Land?

Not necessarily.

For the same questions apply to us today. We pray for Hashem to terminate the *Galut* three times a day, but is that what we truly want?

Jews today comprise many divergent and distinct groups, especially in the religious sectors. Even among the Orthodox, there is a multiplicity of sects, each one absolutely convinced that it, and it *alone*, represents "true Judaism."

Ironically, very often the divisions revolve around minor issues, such as garb, customs, and relatively trivial practices whose importance has been blown out of all proportion. Jews have a knack for taking insignificant religious *behaviors* and treating them as if they are matters that fall into the category of commandments "for which one must die rather than violate."

Thus, religiosity, like politics, becomes a basis for divisiveness and *baseless hatred*, rather than a catalyst for great unity and love.

The Jewish people sometimes appears like a collection of disparate tribes, none of which can see any value beyond their immediate parochial needs and *wants* who display no concern for the *greater good*.

This mentality persists, even in Israel, today. Certain religious groups exert great political influence, directed at obtaining their narrow parochial interests.

However, there is a point where one must yield selfishness in favor of the *good of the nation*. Instead, these groups threaten and often take actions to *weaken* the bonds that unite the Jewish people.

The pursuit of narrow partisan concerns, even religious ones, at the expense of national welfare, is especially dangerous for a country like Israel, which is besieged by lethal enemies and simply cannot afford inner hatred and strife.

This was the flaw at the heart of the rebellions that took place in the wilderness. The people were unable to rise above selfish desires and develop an appreciation for the ideal of *Klal Yisrael* (the community of Israel), which so inspired Moses and which he tried to communicate to his father-in-law. It filled *him* with enthusiasm and longing to lead the people into the Land and to fashion them into a *Kingdom of Priests* (Exodus 19:6).

Moses was genuinely dedicated to the great value of national cohesion. To attain this, one needs to sacrifice partisan

Beha'alotcha

interests when they threaten the fabric of the nation. Moses' attitude was not sufficiently embraced by the people. Unfortunately, he was forced to contend with the *factionalism* that led to the catastrophe of the spies and ultimately to the Exile. The ultimate tragedy was that as a result of the people's contentiousness and provocations, Moses was barred from leading them into *Eretz Yisrael*.

The Rabbis say that, had Moses led the Jews into the Land, he would have built the Holy Temple, and it would never have been destroyed. His unique ability to use Torah to unite the Jews in a spirit of friendship and love would have produced lasting consequences.

We must strive to emulate his example. We must resolve not to allow our religiosity to become a source of division and hatred. We must always be committed to the good of the Jewish nation and be prepared to yield personal agendas in favor of its welfare.

Rebellion in the Wilderness

Parsaht Beha'alotcha concludes the first phase of Jewish existence after the Exodus. Hashem's intention was to bring the people into the land He had promised the Patriarchs, but not until certain objectives were met.

To become the Jewish nation, with its unique mission, the Jews had to encounter the Creator on Mount Sinai and receive His Torah. Then they had to construct a Tabernacle, according to His exact instructions, which would serve as a permanent "abode" of His "presence." When these tasks were completed, there was no further reason to tarry in the wilderness.

The tribes were then arrayed according to the positions they would assume while traveling. All the details pertaining to the Levites' duties in transporting the *Mishkan* were conveyed. The time had come to embark on the great journey to the Holy Land. However, nothing in life goes as smoothly as we would like or expect.

Beha'alotcha

Suddenly, and seemingly out of nowhere, a rebellion broke out. It began with the people grumbling and pining about their *sad* plight. This was a case of extreme self-pity and regret at having to endure the absence of creature comforts and the other deprivations of a sojourn in the desert. This type of speech was highly displeasing to Hashem and a punishment was visited upon them.

However, the matter did not end there. Rashi notes that the motive behind the negative speech was to seek a pretext with which to separate themselves from allegiance to Hashem. The subsequent narrative seems to corroborate this view. Very quickly, a full-fledged insurrection broke out on the matter of *food*. For some inexplicable reason, the people voiced disgust with the *manna* and yearned for the wonderful delicacies they had consumed in Egypt, free.

At first glance, it is impossible to make sense out of this strange behavior. The Torah attests to the superior quality of the *manna*. As a food specifically created by Hashem, it was a nutritionist's dream. It provided for all of one's caloric needs and was completely absorbed in the body with no waste.

It had a very pleasant appearance and taste, and was readily available with little exertion. All the people had to do was go for a light stroll, and they would find it neatly arranged, every day.

One would think that there would be no basis for complaint about these culinary arrangements. Yet, astoundingly, the people took issue with this ideal fare and brazenly declared, "Who will give us meat?" (Numbers 11:4).

They then proceeded to extol the wonderful dishes they had consumed in Egypt and disparaged the *manna* that was Hashem's special gift. How's that for gratitude? Can we make sense of this outrageous behavior?

Consider the strange timing of this uproar. All the preparations for the journey had been made. Moses had joyously proclaimed to his father-in-law, "We are traveling to the land which Hashem has promised to give us..." (Numbers 10:29). It should certainly not have been a time for complaints. In fact, the joyful anticipation of their exciting future should have overshadowed all preoccupation with minor inconveniences.

Yet it did not. Rather, the prospect of entering Canaan brought forth negative emotions and triggered a series of irrational behaviors that culminated in the calamity of the spies.

We can now understand Rashi's comment that, in their initial grumbling, the Jews were seeking a pretext to escape from the demands of the Torah. The imminent trek to Canaan aroused fear and misgivings.

Strange as it seems, they had become accustomed to their life in Egypt and found it difficult to change. People have a great need for security and a debilitating fear of the unknown.

Their reminisces about the wonderful foods of Egypt indicate that they questioned whether Canaan was as lush and bountiful as the land they had left. We may also surmise that they were worried about the battles they would inevitably face. They knew that the land was occupied by fearsome nations who would not take kindly to their plans of conquest.

There was no sin in harboring these fears. They were at fault because they placed the blame on extraneous factors instead of honestly acknowledging their feelings. The Jews could not admit the truth about what really bothered them. They needed an outlet for their discontents, so they complained about food and griped about losing the "wonderful" conditions they had enjoyed in Egypt.

Beha'alotcha

There is an important lesson to be learned here. We must not automatically believe our feelings. Rather, we must challenge and analyze strange emotions that have no basis in reality.

We must have the courage and fortitude to honestly confront our inner nature. Deceiving ourselves into a distorted understanding of the problem can only make matters worse.

Hashem is always there to help us, but we must have the clarity and perspective to evaluate and appreciate His manifold blessings.

Our *True* Pride

Parshat Beha'alotcha describes the state of the Jews as they completed their wilderness tasks and prepared for the imminent conquest of *Eretz Yisrael*. Things begin on a high note, as seen in Moses' enthusiastic invitation to his father-in-law, Jethro, to join him in the invasion and settlement of the land that Hashem had promised to the Jews. "Come with us," Moses exhorted him, "And it shall be... that the goodness with which Hashem shall benefit us, we will do good to you" (Numbers 10:29).

According to Rabbi Soloveitchik, this was an auspicious moment. He asserts that, had Moses led the Jews into Israel, he would have been anointed as *Moshiach* (the Messiah) and built the *Beit Hamikdash*, which would have endured forever. There would have been no exile and dispersion, and the course of Jewish history would have been totally different.

But things did not work out that way. Even Moses could not anticipate what lay just around the corner. Suddenly,

Beha'alotcha

the great leader was beset by a series of rebellions that culminated in the fatal incident of the spies. This brought the forward movement of the Jews to a halt and delayed the conquest for 40 years.

The troubles began with the *mitonenim*, a group of people who grumbled about the conditions they had to endure in the Wilderness. This was soon followed by the provocation of the *Safsuf* (rabble), who complained about the diet of *manna* that Hashem miraculously provided for the people.

The Torah describes how easy it was to obtain this food. "The people would stroll and gather it, and grind it in a mill or pound it in a mortar and cook it in a pot or make it into cakes, and its taste was like the taste of dough kneaded with oil" (Numbers 11:8). Incredibly, the people spurned this perfectly designed sustenance that satisfied all their nutritional needs.

Instead, they were seized with a yearning for meat and longingly recounted the idyllic condition they enjoyed in Egypt where they "sat by the fleshpots" and consumed "fish (free of charge), cucumbers, melons, leeks, onions, and garlic" (Numbers 11:5).

The people's sinful behavior profoundly affected Moses. Instead of defending and praying for them, as he had done in seemingly worse situations, he expressed his frustration and desire to be relieved from his leadership.

Moses begged Hashem to exempt him from this impossible responsibility, uttering words that seem strange and require elucidation. He said to Hashem, "Why have you done evil to your servant; why have I not found favor in Your eyes that You place the burden of this entire people upon me? Did I conceive this entire people or did I give birth to it, that You say to me, 'Carry them in your bosom, as a nurse carries a suckling, to the Land that You swore to its forefathers?" (Numbers 11:11-12).

How are we to understand these words?

Rabbi Soloveitchik explains that the sin of the "complainers" was worse than that of the Golden Calf, because this represented a descent into instinctual lusting and pleasure seeking. The *manna*, by contrast, represents the Jewish lifestyle of *Holiness*, marked by discipline, self-restraint and adhering to boundaries in the pursuit of pleasure. The complainers wanted to remove all barriers to desire, to be free to live a life of endless indulgence, not only regarding food, but other carnal gratification as well.

Moshe realized that his style of leadership as the teacher of the Jewish people was no longer viable. The nation had regressed to the level where they needed "nursing mothers" who would work with them on a personal, emotional basis to slowly wean them away from their sensual "addictions" and gradually raise them to a higher plane.

Moses recognized that he was unsuited for this and could not carry this burden alone. In response to Moses's heartfelt plea, Hashem appointed a group of seventy distinguished elders to share the task of leadership with him.

But something was lost which could not be replaced. This generation would not be able to enter the Promised Land. Of course, officially the verdict would come as a result of the sin of the spies, but the seeds of dissent had already been planted. The Divine plan for the Jews who left Egypt to attain complete redemption by entering *Eretz Yisrael*, with Moses at their head, would not be realized.

That was not only a personal tragedy for Moses. It meant that he would not become *Moshiach* or redeem Israel and the world. Instead, the course of human and Jewish history

Beha'alotcha

would be marked by all the strife, hatred, and massive destruction that we have known and which still prevails.

It is important for us to learn the lessons of Parshat Beha'alotcha, for the Jews are anointed as God's teachers of mankind. To do so, we must represent not only the true ideas of Torah, but its lifestyle of *kedusha*, which is rooted in modesty, restraint and acceptance of limitations in the realm of sexual behavior, as well.

The prophet Balaam noticed this beautiful characteristic of the Jewish people. He said, "How goodly are your tents O Jacob, your dwelling places, O Israel" (Numbers 24:5). This is the *true* national *pride* of the Jewish People. (And not the *false* one that has been paraded in *Yerushalayim* and Tel Aviv.) May we merit to reflect the genuine holiness of Am Yisrael.

SHELACH

The Sin of the Spies: Excessive Guilt

Absolute Faith in Hashem's Promise

The Spies

Sin of the Spies

The Sin of the Spies: Excessive Guilt

The Book of Bamidbar recounts a series of disasters that afflicted the Jews in the Wilderness. After reaching spiritual heights through the national achievement of constructing and dedicating the *Mishkan*, events took a negative turn. Rebellions over food and Moses' leadership broke out.

However, the worst calamity was the episode of the spies. As a result of this debacle, the Jews came to the brink of annihilation, and only Moses' intense prayer appeased God's wrath. However, the punishment was severe and tragic.

The generation that was enslaved, and was freed during the Exodus, and that entered the covenant by receiving the Torah on Mount Sinai, would not live to inherit the Promised Land. Instead they were condemned to wander in the Wilderness for 40 years, until all who had been slaves in Egypt had perished. Their children, who had been spared that debilitating experience, would have the privilege of conquering God's chosen land.

Slavery is one of the worst atrocities, for it inflicts a potentially irreversible wound on the psyche. In spite of all that God had done for them during the Exodus, the Jews could not overcome their slave mentality and assume the role of conquerors.

After all these centuries, do we still, on some level, have a subservient attitude? Is Israel a truly proud and independent country, or does it manifest undue fear of the unjustified condemnation of world opinion? My own sense is that Israel sometimes makes dangerous concessions, releases murderous terrorists, and fails to assert its rights because of an excessive need to curry favor with other nations.

We must seek a deeper understanding of the tragedy of the spies. They brought back a report of the great size and power of the inhabitants, saying that there was no way the Jews could overcome these mightier nations, and that trying to fight them would be suicidal.

While their assessment was correct according to the laws of nature, it omitted the crucial element of Divine assistance. Normally, one is not permitted to rely on miracles. However, in this case, they had God's express guarantee that He would be with them.

It is difficult to understand what caused the national meltdown. Numerous times, the Jews had experienced, firsthand, the power of Divine intervention. They witnessed the plagues that brought Egypt to its knees and the annihilation of its army at the Red Sea. Many other miracles occurred in the Wilderness. So why would they lose faith in God's ability to destroy the physically superior giants who inhabited the Land?

Shelach

Why couldn't God annihilate them as He had done to the mighty Egyptian expeditionary force?

To answer this, we must listen to the words the people uttered. In despair, they said, "Because of Hashem's hatred for us, did He take us out of Egypt to deliver us to the Amorites to destroy us" (Deuteronomy 1:27). It is mind boggling that the Jews could actually make such a claim. Is it possible that sane people could assert that after all the good that Hashem had done for them that His ultimate purpose in delivering them from Egypt was to destroy them? Such thinking seems clearly psychotic!

The great commentator Sforno explains that the people believed they were not worthy to conquer the Land by virtue of God's miracles. Looking within, they remembered their past sins, when they slid into idol worship in Egypt. Although they had repented, they could not rid themselves of their deep-seated guilt. They were fixated on the notion that they were deserving of punishment for past sins and automatically assumed that any attempt to conquer the land was doomed.

The case of the spies contains essential lessons for us. Sometimes people lose faith in God only because they have lost faith in *themselves*. This condition can be brought about when a person has sinned and suffers from excessive guilt. This often engenders a sense of low self-esteem and a belief that one is deserving of harsh punishment. Such a distorted view of reality can seriously undermine one's relationship to the Creator.

This is not to say that guilt or conscience is a necessarily bad thing. In fact, feelings of shame and regret are vital to man's spiritual well-being. Hashem created them because they serve a necessary purpose. A sense of guilt serves

The Sin of the Spies: Excessive Guilt

as a brake on unbridled instinctual indulgence and can be the most potent factor in attaining a righteous existence. However, the human conscience, if not properly utilized, can produce devastating consequences, as well.

It is vitally important to remember that emotions of guilt are not infallible. They should be treated as a sign that you *may* have done something wrong, but just because you *feel* sinful doesn't mean that you *are* sinful.

When a person feels guilty, he should not automatically surrender. Rather, he should use his mind to objectively examine the matter, in order to determine if he has acted wrongfully. Perhaps he should also seek out spiritual advisers who are more objective than he can be in a matter involving himself.

If he discovers that he has sinned, he should not despair and believe he is doomed. He should not become an enemy of himself. He should approach the matter of sin in a rational manner and resist yielding to a sense of *gloom*.

Above all, he must know that all is not lost. For the Torah promises that he can do *teshuva*. When it comes to *spiritual return*, the Torah is very generous to the sinner. The Rambam says that there is *no* sin which is beyond the power of *teshuva*. Indeed, this Sage teaches that the egregious sinner who abandons his evil path and returns faithfully to the service of Hashem is on a higher level than the righteous person who never sinned.

The story of the spies contains important lessons regarding the proper conduct of our religious life. The bulk of our spiritual energy is generally dedicated toward avoiding wrongdoing and acting morally. But we must always remember that no one is perfect and the possibility of sinning always looms.

Shelach

It is important for us to have the fortitude not to be crushed by sin. If we don't yield to our emotions but adhere to the teachings of Torah in this challenging matter, we will learn how we can extricate ourselves from transgression and move on to an even higher level in the service of God. May we merit Divine assistance in this vital endeavor.

Absolute Faith in Hashem's Promise

Parshat Shelach recounts the story of the spies. This episode proved to be a great disaster that almost brought an end to the Jewish people. The "anger" of God flared against them and, as in the case of the Golden Calf, it was only Moses's prayerful intervention that saved the day.

Interestingly, while the initiative for the spying mission came from the people, Moses affirmed it. According to Rashi, Hashem neither endorsed nor rejected it. He instructed Moses to make the decision himself (Rashi on Numbers 13:2). Moses believed it to be a good idea and organized the project.

Again we see that humans, even the greatest of them, are limited and therefore prone to error. This should caution us to keep things in perspective and never overestimate people, even those on the highest level of wisdom and morality.

What was the purpose of the mission on which the spies embarked? It did not seem to be purely a spying operation. Rav Soloveitchik says that there was no need for a

Shelach

reconnaissance team to evaluate the route the invaders were to take. Throughout the trek in the wilderness, the cloud guided the Jews by day, and the pillar of fire by night. This divine "GPS" system led them wherever they were to go and was quite adequate to chart the course of the invasion.

What, then, was the spies' purpose? As we study the text, it becomes clear that they should be regarded more as scouts than as spies. Proof of this is the fact that Moses chose 12 people for this mission, one from each tribe. This is way too many people for a exclusively military reconnaissance mission. Indeed, just prior to the invasion of Canaan, Joshua would send only two stealthy men to obtain needed combat information. However, if the objective of the mission was not limited to matters of war, the size of the unit makes more sense.

Moses's most prominent instruction was to bring back a report about the land, its climate, topography, and natural resources. He even directed them to return with samples of the land's fruit. The scouts were engaged in an agricultural survey to ascertain the viability of the land and its ability to provide sustenance for its inhabitants.

Why was such a mission needed?

Hashem commanded the Jews to "go up and conquer" the land (Deuteronomy 1:21). This was the most difficult challenge the people had confronted since the Exodus from Egypt. They had witnessed the great miracles that Hashem had wrought at the Red Sea. They had summoned the courage to fight off Amalek's attack. They had absolute faith in God's promise.

However, the challenge of conquest was substantially greater. When people have no choices, and their backs are against the wall, they will fight to the death to defend themselves and their families. But it is not, generally, in their nature to launch an offensive against someone who has not attacked them. The Jews did not have a "conqueror's mentality," nor did they view themselves as champions who could uproot a people from their homeland and take it over for themselves. The Jews did not view themselves as worthy of this distinction.

Moses recognized the problem. I believe he hoped that the mission would accomplish two objectives: to alleviate fears about the mythical characteristics of the warriors who resided in Canaan, and, to whet their appetites for this goodly land by a firsthand report of its great qualities, as demonstrated by the fruit samples.

Unfortunately, the adventure proved to be a disaster. Moses had underestimated the great fear the people harbored about the conquest. They could not overcome their sense of inferiority and belief that they were unworthy to inherit this land.

They were thus emotionally predisposed to finding fault and exaggerating any problems they might find. Fear is contagious, and the spies succeeded in transmitting their sense of panic to the hearts of the people.

The Jews' seemingly reasonable need to "see for themselves" may have been a ruse to cover their fear and reluctance to fight against giants. Sometimes it is better to have total trust in Hashem and forget about the hazards.

The Rabbis teach that we are not to calculate the advent of *Moshiach*. All such efforts are doomed to failure. We must have absolute conviction that he will come, because God has given us His promise. It matters not how remote his advent may seem. We must have total and unequivocal faith in the Word of Hashem.

The Spies

Parshat Shelach describes the debacle of the *spies*, which sealed the fate of the generation that experienced the Exodus from Egypt, and generated consequences that affect us to this day. It is important to seek a deeper understanding of this calamity and grasp its appropriate lessons.

First, why was there a need for spies in the first place? The Book of *Devarim* (Deuteronomy) recounts that when Moses issued the order to "go up and inherit the Land," the people came to him and requested that scouts be sent to search out the terrain to determine "the path on which we should ascend and the cities we should conquer" (Deuteronomy 1:21-22). The idea found favor with Moses who, in consultation with Hashem, appointed the leaders of the twelve tribes and delineated their mission.

Interestingly, the mandate of the spies was not limited to obtaining specifically military information. Moses instructed them to report on the agricultural character of the land, its topography and climate. He even urged them to bring back a sampling of the fruits so the people could see for themselves what a choice place this was.

The reconnaissance mission turned out to be a disaster because it induced paralyzing fear in the hearts of the people. And of course, the spies, except for Joshua and Caleb, are regarded as great sinners.

However, it pays to be attentive to the initial words in the report of the scouts. They began by praising the rich quality of *Eretz Yisrael*, affirming that it "flowed with milk and honey" and displayed its choice fruits (Numbers 13:27). Then they said, "However, the nation that dwells there is strong, and its fortified cities are very large, and the descendants of *Anak* (an ancient race of giants) we have seen there" (Numbers 13:28). This statement stimulated the fear that eventually became a massive national panic.

The great commentator Ramban asks, what was sinful about the message of the spies? Weren't they supposed to give an accurate account of what they had seen? Should they have distorted the assessment to make it more palatable? That would clearly have been a violation of their vital mission to bring totally honest information on the matters Moses had delineated. So, what was the sin of the spies?

In my opinion, the problem was that they violated the terms of their assignment and usurped the boundaries of their authority. This type of behavior is very prevalent in our time and has enormous negative consequences. For example, the proper role of a physician is to treat the ill and to preserve life wherever possible. Doctors' expertise lies exclusively in the practice of medicine and the alleviation of human disease.

The question of *when* life begins and whether it can be terminated because of very compelling circumstances, in what

Shelach

is known as *physician assisted suicide*, is *outside* the realm of medical jurisdiction. Doctors have no more authority or professional insight into this matter than ordinary laymen. However, physicians are typically accorded credibility in these areas that they do not deserve. *When* life begins or may be taken away are very complicated moral and religious issues that are wholly outside the subject of medicine.

One who is charged with a mission must know its objective and the limits of his authority. Moses carefully laid out the assignment of the spies. They were to *gather information* regarding the layout of the land and its bounty. They were to bring this information back to Moses who, alone, would decide how to use it.

However, the purpose of the reconnaissance mission was *not* to be the basis of determining whether to go ahead with the conquest or not. That decision had been made by Hashem and was not subject to negotiation. The purpose of the spying was to formulate the best way to carry out the Divine charge to go up and conquer the land.

The sin of the spies was that they *changed* the character of the mission and decided to make it the basis of determining whether it was feasible to fulfill Hashem's command. They usurped their authority and caused devastating consequences.

But did they not speak the truth? The Ramban explains that they employed great cleverness. The Hebrew word for "however" (in the statement "However, the nation is strong...") is *efes* which means, literally, "nothing." With their clever use of innuendo, they were communicating that, yes, the land was very good, but it was all for *nothing* (*efes*), because the people there were so powerful and gigantic that they would slaughter us.

The Spies

By their subtle manipulation of words, the spies exploited the emotional vulnerability of the people-- because they had decided that their task was to make the assessment as to whether it was possible for the Jews to disinherit the land's inhabitants.

This lesson has great relevance in our time, especially in Israel. Military experts have great influence in this country because of the great challenges to its security. However, there is a very thin line between military and political issues, and quite often it is blurred. There is a tradition of former generals entering politics, and this doesn't always work out well. The Oslo Agreement, which has been responsible for so much devastation, was negotiated by a former Chief of Staff. Similarly, the *hitnatkut* (withdrawal) from Gaza, which has become a Hamas launching pad for missiles and terror tunnels on Israel's southern border, was orchestrated by the hero of the Yom Kippur War.

Generals' expertise is in the conduct of battle. The decision get into a war is not a *military,* but a *political* one. So too is the issue of negotiation with the Arab enemies. Questions pertaining to "land for peace" and the "two-state solution" are political matters, and leaders of the Army are not especially qualified to deal with them. Sadly, the record shows that when these people decide that they should be the ones assuming responsibility for areas in which they have no special expertise, tragic results can ensue.

This brings me to the matter of the status of the *Har Habayit* (Temple Mount), which is the *holiest* place in Israel and the one *most* suited for prayer. There are areas where we may not ascend, according to Torah Law, because we are all in a stare of ritual impurity. However, there are certain places where expert *halachic* opinion holds that we may visit.

Shelach

Those who wish to do so are categorically prohibited from even uttering a word of prayer, because the Arab administrators of the site will not allow it. The Jews have always longed to return to *Yerushalayim* and all its holy places. When East Jerusalem was under Jordanian control, Jewish cemeteries were desecrated and Jews could not visit the *Kotel* (Western Wall).

All that changed in June 1967, when heroic Israeli soldiers shed much blood and fought gruesome battles to liberate the Old City and its holy places. Who can forget the immortal words of Commander Motta Gur, who simply said, "*Har Habayit beyadeinu*" (The Temple Mount is in our hands)?

Sadly, it was not for long. On that same day, Defense Minister Moshe Dayan, one of Israel's military legends, made a misbegotten *political* decision to restore the "status quo" by returning control over the Temple Mount to the Jordanian religious authority known as the *Waqf*, who ruled that only Moslems could pray there; anyone of a different religion could not recite any religious supplications in that place.

A crucial decision such as that should *not* have been made by a Defense Minister. It should have been made by the government, which would have considered *all* the implications, especially the impact on religious Jews, and hopefully have come to a more just resolution. At the very least, the right of Jews to not only visit, but to also pray at their holiest site, should have been guaranteed.

It goes without saying that the generosity of Mr. Dayan was neither reciprocated or appreciated. He was a great military leader making a major decision in an area *outside* his scope of expertise. This was the sin of the spies. The syndrome afflicts us to this day. We must be cognizant of it and guard against it.

Sin of the Spies

Parshat Shelach recounts the tragic story of the spies. The Torah is scrupulously honest and clearly details the sins of even the most righteous people. The protagonists here were 12 tribal leaders selected by God for this exploratory mission. Moses directed them to search out the military features of the land, as well as its demographic and agricultural qualities.

The expedition turned into a fiasco when the spies encountered the mighty giants who were native to the land. They were overcome by paralyzing fear and conspired to induce a panic in the Jews that would prevent them from embarking on the conquest.

The story of the spies is difficult to comprehend. These were righteous men who, presumably, had witnessed Hashem's miracles and had faith in His promises. If He was with them, what difference did it make how mighty the inhabitants of the land were?

Let us seek to understand the mindset of the spies. They most certainly must have assumed their responsibilities

Shelach

with the best of intentions. However, as they explored the land, they were struck by the fearsome appearance of the natives and were smitten with terror. They believed that the people were being led to their doom.

All people, no matter how great, are only human and thus subject to emotion. So we can understand that the spies could be overwhelmed by panic at the sight of scary looking giants. Such a thing occurred years later when the Philistine warrior, Goliath, emerged from the enemy ranks and challenged any Jewish soldier to take him on, *mano a mano*. He mocked and degraded the Jews and their God day after day, yet all were struck by fear, and no one stepped forth to accept the challenge and terminate the disgrace. That is, until David came by, saw and understood what was transpiring, and stood up for Israel.

The sin of the spies is not that they were overcome by fear. No one can control all his immediate emotional responses. The transgression lay in their actions. They should have acknowledged that they felt extreme trepidation and were not capable of discharging their task in a rational manner.

They should have approached Moses, told him what had happened to them, and asked him to excuse them from their mission. Had they revealed their true emotional state to Moses, there is no doubt that he would have been sympathetic and removed them from their positions. The whole debacle of the spies would have been avoided! What prevented them from adopting this rational course?

We can learn a significant lesson from this story. A person must have substantial self-knowledge to attain genuine righteousness. This is especially true for those who have cultivated a self-image of goodness and faithfulness that is not entirely in line with reality.

They may find themselves in a crisis in which a hitherto unseen emotional resistance now manifests itself. Are they prepared to acknowledge their weakness and have their image shattered, or do they seek ways to avoid this?

The sin of the spies was their inability to recognize their personal flaw and confess it to Moses. All they had to do was to admit that they were not capable of discharging the assignment and needed to be replaced by other more stalwart individuals. Instead, they deflected the blame outward, disparaging the land and asserting that it "consumed its inhabitants." They pretended that the problem did not lie within them, but in the land itself.

It is very important for us to accurately assess our own capabilities. We need to avoid the temptation to adopt a self-image that is not in line with our actual character. A mistaken sense of self might tempt us into accepting responsibilities that are beyond our level of competence, and this can lead to terrible setbacks.

Above all, we must be extremely honest in acknowledging our weaknesses, when ignoring them could have devastating consequences. Losing face is painful, but it is a small price to pay to preserve our integrity and righteousness.

KORACH

Korachism

What a Difference a Friend Makes

Popularity is Ephemeral

The Hidden Blessing Within the Curse

The True Teachers of Torah

Rebellion

Korachism

One of the most inspiring aspects of Torah is its scrupulous honesty. It never hides even the most unseemly occurrences. It records, for the sake of truth, unsavory incidents we would rather had not taken place. Inevitably, this prompts us to revise and purify our understanding of human nature and the conflicts we must overcome in our attempts to reach a higher level of perfection in the service of God.

Parshat Korach describes a rebellion which was launched against Moses by a coalition consisting of his cousin Korah and a group of *malcontents* which he had cobbled together. The Rabbis of the Talmud discerned that the movement had both political and theological ramifications.

On the overt level, Korah posed as a champion of the people, accusing Moses of amassing power by assuming the leadership and appointing Aaron, his brother, as the High Priest. Thereby, Moses had seized control of the nation's supreme theological and governmental offices. Korah argued that "the entire community is holy, and God is among them, so why do you raise yourself over the congregation of Hashem?" (Numbers 16:3).

We are astounded at the brazenness of Korah and his blatant distortion of Moses's character. Moses was the most humble of men and had pleaded to be excused from the task of leadership, for which he felt unqualified. God overruled him and chose him to be the leader precisely because he harbored no craving for power.

His achievements in leading the Jews out of Egypt and giving them the Torah did not go to his head. When the people bombarded him with their lust for meat, Moses entreated Hashem to establish a governing body with whom he could share power. He would have preferred to relinquish his position to humbly teach Torah and minister to those in need.

Given the evidence of Moses's humility, what prompted Korah to make such outrageous accusations?

Rashi explains that Korah, at first, accepted Moses's appointment of Aaron, for he believed he would be designated as prince of their tribe, Levi. When, due to his character flaws, Korah was bypassed, he was enraged and resolved to challenge Moses.

Thus, this "champion of democracy" was, in reality, a frustrated power seeker.

Moses understood the egotistical motives behind the actions of Korach. He responded to Korah's charges by reminding him of the special privileges he enjoyed as a Levite and said, "Is it not enough that God has separated you to minister before Him, and you seek also the priesthood?" (Numbers 16: 9). Korach was guilty of projecting his own lust for power onto Moses.

According to the Rabbis, Korah and his cohorts also rebelled against the Halachic system, which spelled out the manner of performing the commandments. They laughed at Moses when he ruled that a house filled with Torah scrolls nevertheless requires a mezuzah. Logic dictates, they said, that if a tiny parchment with three paragraphs suffices for a house, certainly an abode filled with sacred writings should not need a mezuzah.

They maintained, in other words, that ordinary common sense should be the deciding factor in Jewish practice.

Judaism, however, is based on the Written Law, as interpreted and elucidated by the Oral Law-- which was taught to Moses on Sinai and transmitted by the greatest Torah scholars from generation to generation, up to the present day. Whoever desires to observe the Torah as revealed by God *must* follow the teachings of the "Masters of the Oral Law" who are the disciples of Moses.

The rebellion of Korah is not just a matter of historical interest. In every generation, we are confronted with new manifestations of Korachism, i.e., the desire to remake Judaism to conform to prevailing attitudes.

Contemporary society is going through monumental change. Traditional values in vital areas such as marriage, family, sexual behavior, and sanctity of life have been deemed irrelevant and obsolete. This has created tremendous pressure on Jewish religious leaders to modify the Torah in accordance with the values of the time.

There has arisen, in our time, many modern spiritual "descendants" of Korah who rise up to challenge the authentic Torah teachings based on the Oral Law, whose goal is to appeal to contemporary moral sensitivities. We need to differentiate between genuine Torah leaders who courageously resist the tide of the times and are selflessly dedicated to preserving God's Torah and those who masquerade their desire for power behind attractive slogans and popular agendas.

It is vitally important for every Jew to reaffirm his belief that *Moshe emet v'Torato emet* (Moses is true and his Torah is true) (Talmud Bava Batra 74a). We must insist that anyone who assumes a position of religious leadership be scrupulously faithful to elucidating and defending the Torah of Moshe. We must categorically reject an *alien* Torah which reflects the mindset of the innovators but is not the teaching of our classic Talmudic authorities.

It is only by courageously adhering to the eternal truths of our religious heritage, no matter how unpopular, that we can be a "Light unto the Nations" (Isaiah 49:6). May we merit to achieve this.

What a Difference a Friend Makes

Parshat Korach recounts the story of a rebellion orchestrated by a distinguished group of leaders against Moses's authority and the legitimacy of the appointments he had made.

Korah and his cohorts argued that it was wrong for Moses to select his brother, Aaron, and his descendants to be the *Kohanim* who, alone, had the right to perform the Temple service. Korah, one of Moses's cousins, was a Levite and thus eligible to assist the *Kohanim* and perform "secondary" services in the Temple.

However, Korah did not find this to be satisfactory and took umbrage at being excluded from the primary activities of ministering before God. Thereupon, Korah organized a group of 250 major Torah scholars who found common cause with his insurrection.

What a Difference a Friend Makes

Most of these people were from the tribe of Reuven, who was Yaakov's *bechor*. Originally, the firstborn males were slated to do the Temple service, but this privilege was revoked when they participated in the sin of the Golden Calf.

Korah's uprising was the third major rebellion that occurred in the Wilderness. The first, which we read about in Beha'alotcha, was a protest against the *manna*, and had tragic consequences. The second was the rebellion of the Spies, who instigated the people to disobey the command to "go up and conquer" (Deuteronomy 1:8) the land of Israel.

This resulted in the Divine decree that the generation of the Exodus would not inherit the country that "flowed milk and honey" (Numbers 13:27). Instead, they would wander for 40 years until all of them passed away.

According to the Ramban, it was the debacle of the Spies that unleashed Korah's dispute. His anger and jealousy had been aroused some time before, when Aaron received his appointment. However, he did not act immediately, but held his emotions in check because of the tremendous popularity that Moses then enjoyed.

Moses was extremely beloved by the people because he was always there for them to perform great miracles of salvation in Egypt and in the Wilderness. After the Egyptian army was utterly destroyed, the people "believed in Hashem and His servant Moses" (Exodus 14:31).

He was their champion in whom they had total confidence. They came to rely on him so much that when he was late in returning from the mountain, they, tragically, prevailed on Aaron to fashion something which would serve as a substitute for their great leader.

Moses's aura was enhanced when he successfully interceded with Hashem to save them from destruction after

Korach

the sin of the Golden Calf. Moses had reached the zenith of his popularity, and any attempt to challenge his legitimacy would have been firmly quashed. Korah knew this and patiently bided his time.

Finally, Moses's popularity plummeted when he could not prevent the decree that, because of the sin of the Spies, the people would spend 40 years wandering in the Wilderness and die without entering the Promised Land. Korah realized that *this* was his moment to strike.

We can learn a great deal from Korah. When he felt affronted, he could not act immediately, and thus had time to reconsider the action he was contemplating. At various points in our lives, we may find ourselves in a similar situation. We have a powerful grievance but, for the moment, can't do anything about it. What should we do in the interim?

Many people have absolute confidence in the veracity of their feelings and are not inclined to challenge their beliefs. A wise person takes a different approach. He knows that emotions, especially very compelling ones, are deceptive. He doesn't blindly trust his innate sense of right and wrong, especially when his ego is involved.

He therefore uses the period of grace in which he cannot act to gain a greater insight into his position. He knows that he cannot do this by himself, but requires the help of an objective outsider. He needs a true friend.

There are two kinds of friends. We instinctively gravitate to someone who shares our outlook on things and is sympathetic to our attitude. This person is there to reassure us about the correctness of our viewpoint and the goodness of our character.

It's nice to have that kind of person in your life, because we all want our feelings to be validated. But is this always beneficial?

What we really need is a *true* friend in whom we can confide and who will be absolutely honest about our words and behavior. Such a person is like a doctor who does not withhold the truth from his patient because, to cure him, he must be brutally honest about his condition.

Pirkei Avot instructs us to "acquire for yourself a friend" (Ethics of Our Fathers 1:6). Rambam explains the different kinds of friendship one can have. The most exalted is the relationship between two people who are absolutely committed to each other's spiritual perfection. This is the person we can turn to for moral guidance in vital matters when we may be blind to our own motivations.

The tragedy of Korah is that he didn't have a true friend. Our parsha begins with the words, "and Korah took…" (Numbers 16:1). Rashi explains that he took himself to one side to contend against Moses. He was absolutely committed to his own position and did not leave open the possibility that he could be wrong. Korah did not have the capacity to transcend his hurt feelings and view things in a different way.

There is so much we can learn from this story. We should assiduously seek to avoid *machloket* (unnecessary strife), especially against great teachers, and strive to cultivate true friends who can be a beacon of light in those moments when our vision is clouded.

Popularity is Ephemeral

Parshat Korach depicts another tragedy in the Wilderness, the rebellion against the integrity of Moses's leadership. He was accused by Korah and his henchmen of arbitrarily allocating the *Kehuna* (priesthood) to his brother Aaron and his descendants in order to amass power and rule over the Jewish nation.

According to the Rabbis, Korah's agitation also extended to the quality of Moses's decisions in the matter of Jewish law. In challenging him on this, he resorted to *mockery*.

As the *Midrash* goes, Korah gathered 250 heads of the Sanhedrin, and they posed *halachic* (legal) queries to Moses. For example, does a house filled with Torah scrolls require a *mezuzah*? When Moses answered in the affirmative, they *laughed* and said, if a small scroll containing two paragraphs of the Torah is sufficient to render a house halachically acceptable, then shouldn't an abode suffused with holy writings be exempt from the *mezuzah*? (Rashi on Numbers 16:1).

There is a dispute between the Ibn Ezra and the Ramban as to *when* this revolt occurred. The former commentator reasons that, since the overt objection of Korah was to the elevation of Aaron, we should assume that it took place when that appointment happened and, therefore, the story is not recounted in its proper chronological order.

The Ramban challenges this view and maintains that the story *is* presented at the time when it occurred, in other words, *after* the tragedy of the spies. He agrees that Korah's motivation was the choice of the *Kohen* (priest), which triggered his ire. However, Korah controlled his anger and did not act immediately, because he was shrewd. He understood that any attempt to depose Moses at that time would have been an exercise in futility.

For when the *Mishkan* was established, Moses was at the height of his popularity. It was a time of effusive national celebration. The people recognized Moses's great accomplishments in taking them out of Egypt, leading them in the wilderness, and bringing them the Torah. Most of all, they understood that no one but *Moses* could have successfully interceded with Hashem to save them from destruction in the matter of the Golden Calf.

Korah was smart and bided his time. He knew that, inevitably, Moses's popularity would wane. He cunningly sensed that his moment had come after the debacle of the spies. Ironically, this calamity resulted in a certain sense of hostility against Moses, even though it was only *his* prayers that, once again, saved the nation.

Still, the punishment for the sin was too great to bear. The generation that had left Egypt would never enter the *Promised Land*, but would die in the Wilderness. This was akin to a sentence of life in prison with no possibility of parole.

Korach

There was nothing for them to do except wander in the desert and wait to die.

There was no future, no goals, no going further to "bigger and better things." They could not be content with or adapt to this decree. Hashem had judged that they were not fit to inherit *Eretz Yisrael*. This was received as a total rejection, and on a certain level, they *blamed* Moses. Why couldn't he rescue us from *this*? The national mood was now a very different one, and Korah struck because he sensed that the moment was propitious. He wasn't wrong.

We must come very sadly to the conclusion that the Jews never grasped or appreciated *Moshe Rabbeinu's true* greatness. Had the people rallied behind him in the Korah "affair," the entire tragedy could have been avoided. Moses's integrity as the absolutely dedicated leader and perfectly *honest* transmitter of the *Mesorah* (Oral Law) was under attack, and the people who had experienced his greatness should have proclaimed with one voice, *"Moshe emet ve'torato emet"* (Talmud Sanhedrin 110a).

Had they done so, the entire course of Jewish history might have been different. We could have been spared from the many secessionist movements and encroachments on *halacha* that plague us to this very day.

We can now recognize the full measure of the consequences of the sin of the spies. It initiated the *dark mood* in which the sin of *makchish magidehah* (denigration of her transmitters) reared its ugly head. There is nothing more tragic than that.

Because Judaism, at bottom, rests entirely on the validity of the *Mesorah* and the inviolability of the *Rebbe-Talmid* (teacher-student) relationship. The cooperative endeavor of the transmitters and receivers of the Oral Tradition is the axis upon which the Jewish way of life revolves.

That is what Korah sought to rend asunder. His injured ego was more vital to him than the preservation of the authentic *Oral Tradition*. The 250 heads of the Sanhedrin were not innocent either. They, more than anyone, should have known how devastating their insurgency would be.

This is a very sobering lesson for all of us. It is wonderful to amass voluminous Torah knowledge. However, if it does not permeate your soul and captivate your heart, it remains *extraneous* and can go to your head, and magnify your ego with ruinous consequences.

Moses, who was the greatest of prophets, was also the most *humble* of men. The Rambam says that the most significant virtue in obtaining true wisdom is *humility*.

Let us strive mightily to attain it, for it is only through humility that we can remove baseless hatred from our midst. And the Torah knowledge it will engender will enable us to reach the level of wisdom where the nations will proclaim of the Jews, "What a wise and discerning nation is this great people" (Deuteronomy 4:6).

The Hidden Blessing Within the Curse

Parshat Korach describes the terrible rebellion against Moses's authority, which was launched by none other than his own cousin.

One cannot imagine a more egregious deed: *Moshe Rabbenu* was the most important person in the Jewish nation. He had qualities that no one else possessed and reached a level of prophecy where God spoke to him "face to face" (Exodus 33:11).

No one else could have performed the mission of redeeming the Jews from Egypt and transforming them into a "kingdom of *Kohanim* (priests) and a holy nation" (Exodus 19:6). Moses alone was capable of receiving the Torah from Hashem and teaching it to the Jewish people.

Aside from his "superhuman" intellectual and prophetic abilities, Moses was also morally perfected. He was the most humble person who had ever lived, and harbored no desire for power or glory. To the contrary, he had an aversion to everything associated with the spotlight.

The Hidden Blessing Within the Curse

It is hard for us to appreciate Moses's greatness, for he spurned all the things an ordinary mortal longs for. As God said in His rebuke of Miriam, "*Not so* my servant Moses; he is the most faithful in My entire house" (Numbers 12:7). Miriam, who meant no harm, was severely punished for criticizing Moses's seemingly inexplicable separation from his wife.

Yet this incident did not chasten Korah, who charged that Moses was guilty of nepotism. He declared that Moses sought to keep all the power in his hands by assigning the priesthood to his brother Aaron and keeping the kingship for himself. This denigration of Moses could have had wide-ranging repercussions.

The accusation that Moses had acted on his own, without instruction from Hashem, had the potential to undermine the whole foundation of Torah *miSinai* (from Sinai) and the absolutely Divine character of the Torah. The revolt of Korah and his cohorts had to be dealt with, in the most forceful way. It had to be made crystal clear that the system of *halacha* originated at Sinai. If the notion that the Rabbis *made up* the laws of the Torah had prevailed, then Judaism, as revealed by God, would been effectively nullified.

There is a debate as to the timing of Korah's rebellion. Some say it happened when Moses designated Aaron as the *Kohen Gadol* at the time the *Mishkan* was consecrated, but is only recounted in Korach. However, the Ramban maintains that the story is in its correct chronological order and that it took place after the disaster of the spies.

The Ramban explains that, although Korah's resentment was aroused when Moses made the priestly appointment, he held his anger in check. At that point, Moses's popularity was at its zenith, because he had taken the Jews out

Korach

of Egypt, split the Red Sea, brought down the Torah, and successfully defended them after the sin of the Golden Calf.

Now, however, Korah sensed that the time to strike was right. Moses's popularity had waned, as many were punished for the sin of "lusting" for meat and, more significantly, for that of the spies. Moses could not prevail upon God to rescind the decree that they would not enter the Promised Land, but would die in the wilderness. Korah therefore believed that widespread discontent would draw the people to his cause.

Indeed, he was successful in winning over some of the most prominent Sages of the time.

Harsh punishments from Hashem were necessary to quell the uprising, but there is another dimension to this tragedy. The decree that the entire generation would die in the wilderness indeed seems very bleak. Imagine, being in a situation where you have nothing to look forward to and know that, within 40 years, it will all be over. Was there a lesson Korah missed, but which we now can learn?

I believe that there might just be a blessing hidden within the Divine curse. God is always merciful, even in punishment. For we should observe that Hashem did not kill that generation immediately, but gave them 40 years. Hashem, in His mercy, gave them the opportunity to "number their days and obtain a heart of wisdom" (Psalms 90:12).

We all live with a fantasy of immortality and believe we will be around forever. This causes us to postpone vital spiritual imperatives and waste tremendous amounts of time.

Hashem's decree was meant to rouse the Jews from their slumber. They could no longer indulge their denial of death. If they were wise, they would galvanize their energies and live every day to its fullest.

The Hidden Blessing Within the Curse

The tragedy of Korah was that, instead of recognizing the reality of death and responding with wholehearted *teshuva*, he persisted with gratifying his baser impulses of anger against Moses. As a result, he wound up losing everything when the possibility of eternal life lay open before him. That is the essence of tragedy.

May we all merit to recognize that "the day is short and the work is long, and the workers are lazy and the reward is great, and the Master of the House is pressing us" (Ethics of Our Fathers 2:20). And, "If not now, when?" (Ethics of Our Fathers 1:14).

The True Teachers of Torah

Parshat Korach describes the pernicious revolt of a group of conspirators against Moses's leadership.

Korah was one of Moses's cousins and *should* have known better, but he did not learn from the mistakes of others. His failure is similar to that for which Rashi condemned the Spies, who spoke evil words about the land of Israel, and did not learn from the transgression of Miriam (Rashi on Numbers 13:2).

Miriam had criticized her brother Moses because he had separated from his wife. Her motives were pure. She bore him no ill will, but genuinely believed that he erred by assuming that his high level of prophecy required that he live a celibate life. However, she *mistakenly* compared herself to Moses, asserting that she and Aaron were also prophets, and yet had not been instructed to cease married life.

In response, Hashem revealed an entire section of Torah that depicted Moses's unique status and the qualitative superiority of his prophecy, which put him in a class by himself.

Miriam's sin was that she did not sufficiently appreciate Moses's high spiritual level, which would have prohibited uninformed speculation about his behavior. Hashem concluded His rebuke of Miriam and Aaron with the words, "How did you not *fear* to speak about my servant, about Moses?" (Numbers 12:8).

It is a wonder that Korah and his cohorts did not learn from Miriam's punishment. Korah attributed serious flaws to Moses, asserting that he was obsessed with the accumulation of power.

Moses had attained supreme political authority by accepting the position of king. And he also retained control over the religious establishment by granting the priesthood to his brother Aaron and his descendants.

Korah claimed that this was an affront to the dignity of the Jews, all of whom should have been allowed to participate in the divine service. He appealed to the liberal and democratic instincts of the people, saying, "for the entire Congregation is holy, and Hashem is among them, so why do you [Moses] exalt yourself over the Assembly of Hashem?" (Numbers 16:3).

The revolt was not limited to Korah. He shrewdly gathered a group of 250 leaders, mainly from the tribe of Reuben. Apparently, that tribe, which descended from Jacob's oldest son, had a residual grievance because the Temple service had been taken from the firstborn and transferred to Moses's tribe, Levi.

According to the Rabbis, the rebels also challenged Moses's halachic authority. They asked "gotcha" questions that sought to make him an object of ridicule. They queried, does a

Korach

tallit (prayer shawl) made entirely of *techelet* (special blue dye) require fringes? Does a house filled with Torah scrolls require a mezuzah? When Moses answered in the affirmative, they laughed (Rashi on Number 16:1).

The rebels exulted in their own cleverness. Isn't the purpose of a mezuzah, they tauntingly implied, to remind us, as we enter our homes, of the existence of the Creator and our duty to love Him? And if, their reasoning went, a tiny parchment with two paragraphs suffices for this, shouldn't a house filled Torah scrolls render the need for a mezuzah superfluous?

What strikes us is the mocking tone of the scoffer's response to Moses's decisions. When he asserted that such a house *does* require a mezuzah, they laughed. That was a laughter of denial and disparagement, expressing their rejection of Moses as the designated interpreter of God's Torah.

The essence of Moses's greatness is that Hashem chose him to draw close to Him and become His servant. He earned this distinction because he was the most humble person and most qualified transmitter of Torah.

The disparagement of genuine Torah authorities did not cease with the demise of Korah and his wicked cohort. It has persisted throughout our history and rears its ugly head to this very day.

Indeed, there are contemporary rabbis, some of whom identify as Orthodox, who rebel against unpopular *halachic* teachings and even sneer at the Torah position on fundamental contemporary religious issues.

Remember, Korah's central contention was false. The Torah was *not* given over to the entire "holy congregation" to be interpreted and applied according to its intrinsic logic and common sense. It was transmitted by Hashem to Moses and his successors, an extremely select group of highly perfected, humble individuals who dedicate their lives to the *accurate* transmission of *Torat Moshe* (the Torah of Moses).

The basic argument of Korah, that all Jews have the ability to offer their own interpretations of Scripture, is very much in line with the contemporary outlook. Our society encourages us to believe that we can be "whatever we want to be," presumably if we only work hard enough at it.

Judaism *does* concur with the view of modern society that "all men are created equal," but that is only in the sense that they are fashioned in the "Image" of God (Genesis 1:27). However, we do not take this to mean that all individuals are equal in terms of intellectual abilities, talents and skill sets. It *only* means that no one can claim that his life is more important than anyone else's. For every human manifests the Divine Image.

The notion that anyone could become an Einstein if he only strove for it with the requisite dedication is patently absurd. The same holds true for every area of human endeavor. There are very few people who could attain the golfing level of Tiger Woods or the basketball capability of Michael Jordan, no matter how much effort they put into that project.

Of course, hard work and discipline can take you a very long way but, ultimately, one cannot achieve things that are outside the range of his potential, which is limited and irrevocable.

We can now understand the 7th Principle of Jewish Faith articulated by Maimonides. After stating that the belief in prophecy is a basic tenet in Judaism, he formulated an additional fundamental relating exclusively to the prophecy of Moses. He said: "We accept that Moses was the father of all Prophets that were before him and that will be after him. He

Korach

was on a qualitatively different level than any other... And he, peace be upon him, rose to the level of the angels. He was granted all areas of knowledge and prophecy and his physical attributes did not diminish. His knowledge was different and it is through this difference that it is ascribed to him that he spoke to God without any intermediary or angel" (Talmud Sanhedrin, Maimonides' commentary on the Mishna).

We are obliged to believe not just in the *general* phenomenon of prophecy but in the *specific* exalted level of the prophetic experience attained by Moses. Moses reached a unique level of intellectual and ethical perfection never duplicated by any other.

This rendered Moses the only one who was qualified to receive the Torah from God and transmit it to the "Masters of the Oral Law." This is an elite group of people who, alone, have the special understanding and dedication to truth that qualifies them to be the *exclusive* transmitters and arbiters of God's Torah, i.e., the Written and Oral Law.

Korah, in point of fact, *denied* the seventh Fundamental principle of Faith as stated by the Rambam. He asserted that there was nothing special about Moses' knowledge and understanding. He maintained that everyone was "Holy" and if they used their own judgement, could interpret the Torah just as well as the Master.

This Parsha contains a great lesson for our generation, specifically directed at those who regard themselves as Judaism's contemporary spiritual leaders.

This lesson is that our leaders have a great role to play in preserving the Jewish People and religion in the stormy times in which we live. The lifestyle changes implemented by modern man and his utter revamping of the traditional moral code has raised some monumental and unprecedented religious issues.

The Rabbis must know that they bear great responsibility in dealing with the many complex challenges that the Jewish community faces. But they must refrain from entering areas that are outside the sphere of their legitimate authority. They should educate and inspire Jews to observe the Torah and minister to their various religious needs.

But they have no qualification to make decisions that must be left to the authentic Masters of the Oral Law. When they venture into matters that lie outside their realm of expertise and seek to modify Jewish doctrines that have been established and confirmed by the foremost Talmudic sages throughout the ages, on earthshaking matters such as homosexuality, abortion, and the like, they assume the position of latter day Korahs.

Torah study is a highly dynamic activity, for which we have been granted great intellectual freedom. We have every right to question, challenge, demand answers, and use our God-given intellects in our quest to understand and appreciate our divine heritage.

But we must remember that it is only *Torat Moshe*, "the inheritance of the congregation of Jacob," (Deuteronomy 33:4) that will endure forever. Let us approach it and its *true* teachers with awe.

Rebellion

Parshat Korach takes up one of the most tragic stories in the Torah, the rebellion against Moses's leadership. It is ironic that the instigator of this insurgency was one of Moses's close relatives, who should have known better.

One wonders, did the Jews not recognize and appreciate the superior qualities of the one who confronted Pharaoh, brought plagues on Egypt, and led the people out of their enslavement? He alone went to the peak of Mount Sinai, where Hashem addressed him directly in the sight of the nation and gave him the *Luchot* (Tablets).

It should have been apparent to the entire people that Moses was in a class by himself. Yet that clearly was not the case. According to Nachmanides, Korah's anger was aroused when Moses appointed Aaron and his descendants to minister in the Temple instead of the *bechorot* (firstborn males).

Korah realized that he would have no chance if he acted immediately, because Moses enjoyed great popularity at that point. So he shrewdly waited for the time when Moses's approval would plummet, and he would become vulnerable to attack.

That opportunity came after the debacle of the spies, for, contrary to the case of the Golden Calf, Moses did not pray for the people, nor did he rescue them from the decree that they would die in the Wilderness. Korah sensed that Moses's overall support had weakened, and he struck.

How is it that the people didn't react with outrage to Korah's charges? Where was the *hakarat hatov* (gratitude) for all the good that Moses had done for them? Could they point to one situation where Moses had acted for personal motives and had disregarded the best interests of the nation?

The assertion that the people were upset with Moses because of the harsh punishment for the sin of the spies is instructive. This indicates that they had not done genuine *teshuva*. For that requires that a person look within and take *full* responsibility for his sinful actions. Had they taken that approach they would never have blamed Moses for *their* failure.

Korah accused Moses of seeking personal aggrandizement by assuming the kingship for himself and appointing his brother to the highest spiritual position in Israel. One must admit that, from a superficial perspective, Aaron's appointment can *seem* to be suspicious. Judges and others in positions of authority are expected to avoid not just actual impropriety, but the very *appearance* of corruption as well. Why then was Aaron's appointment made in a manner that *could* be interpreted as having selfish motivation?

Let us consider Moses's prayer to Hashem not to accept the offering of Dathan and Abiram. Moses said, " ...I did not take a single donkey from them, nor did I harm any one of them" (Numbers 16:15). Rashi comments that, even when he returned to Egypt to assume the leadership and had a

Korach

right to use a communal donkey, still he used his own transportation.

Why *didn't* Moses make use of public funds which would have been perfectly legitimate since he was engaged in community business? Additionally, how does his behavior before he began his mission reflect on actions he took after he was already in a position of power?

In my opinion, Moses was explaining that being the leader was not something he had pursued or desired. He had accepted the mission purely as a service to Hashem, for which he did not expect any restitution from the people he was serving. Many leaders claim that are "serving" the people, while, in truth, the matter is reversed; they view the people as a means to their own enrichment and glory.

Korah did not really comprehend the uniqueness and greatness of Moses. Korah projected onto Moses the qualities of an ordinary leader, who always seeks to increase power. This misconception caused him to interpret the designation of Aaron as an act of nepotism.

Indeed, Aaron's selection constituted a test for *Klal Yisrael*, as well. It challenged them to look deeply into the matter and put aside *appearances* in favor of a sober estimation of Moses's character. Had they done so, they would have realized that Moses was the true *eved Hashem* (servant of God), who carried out His instructions faithfully without any concern for personal gain.

Hashem provided the Jews with the greatest leader in all of history. Indeed, we have been blessed with great Torah leaders of absolutely selfless dedication throughout the generations. Have we, as Jews, perceived and properly acknowledged the righteousness of our superlative but humble leaders?

Rebellion

This is a subject of great importance. Let us pay special attention to the prayer we utter in the *Amidah* (petitionary prayer) regarding this matter: "Bring back our judges as at first and our advisers as in the beginning and remove from us worry and anxiety, and rule over us, You Hashem, alone, with mercy and compassion and exonerate us in judgment. Blessed are you, Hashem, Who loves righteousness and justice."

May we strive to become worthy of our great Torah leaders so that we can learn from their wisdom noble actions. And may we merit to see the day when the rule of Hashem is, once again, upon us.

CHUKAT

Vicarious Atonement?

In the Merit of the Righteous

Do We Respect Other Religions?

The Red Heifer

Death by the Kiss

Vicarious Atonement?

Parshat Chukat begins with the commandment of the Red Heifer, which is followed by the death of Miriam.

It should be noted that there is a gap in the narrative of the sojourn of the Jews in the Wilderness. There is no account of what took place during the 40-year stay in the *Midbar* (desert) that had been decreed, in Parshat Shelach, because of the sin of the spies. All the events recorded in Chukat take place after the culmination of the enforced wandering.

The severe punishment for the sin of the spies illustrates an important Torah lesson, i.e., that the forward momentum of the Jewish people can be stalled, but not halted. That is not to say we are perfect, for we can become corrupt and engage in sinful behavior. But God's chosen people are eternal. Other nations and empires that are subject to the ordinary laws of nature will come and go. Not so the Jews. We are under a special Divine Providence that guarantees our survival.

Vicarious Atonement

Being chosen, however, does not grant us a free pass. Indeed, Hashem demands *more* of us and metes out serious punishment when warranted. Nevertheless, the Jewish nation cannot be eliminated.

This lesson is clearly illustrated in our own time. No people has experienced a greater calamity than the Jews did during the Holocaust. Yet this catastrophe was followed by the establishment of Israel and its development into one of the most advanced societies on earth.

As we have seen, the opening section of Parshat Chukat, which concerns the Red Heifer, is followed by the death of Miriam. Rashi explains that the juxtaposition of these two subjects is to teach us that, just as the Red Heifer provides atonement, so too does the death of the righteous (Rashi on Numbers 19:20).

At first glance, this idea seems very strange. Judaism rejects the notion of "vicarious atonement." This doctrine is contrary to the idea of Divine Justice. Judaism affirms that the "Lord is righteous in all His ways" (Psalms 145:17). Accordingly, God rewards and punishes a person in accordance with his deeds. Just as fathers are not punished for the sins of their sons, the sons are not rewarded for the good deeds of their parents. If one has sinned, he must do sincere *teshuva* and will thus obtain forgiveness. In what sense can it be said that the death of the righteous provides atonement?

A unique feature of Jewish history is the preponderance of *Tzadikim* (righteous people) who have appeared in every time and place of Jewish existence. Our heroes are a unique brand of individuals. They are profound thinkers who devote themselves to Torah study as well as to other branches of knowledge.

Chukat

However, the goal of their study is not mere intellectual satisfaction. They seek to obtain a deeper understanding of Hashem's ways so they can perfect themselves by emulating them.

No other nation can even approach the Jewish record in this regard. The genuine *Talmid Chacham* who devotes himself to study and good deeds is the national treasure of the Jewish people. The Rambam says that the "crown" of Torah is greater than that of the Kingship and Priesthood (Mishneh Torah, Laws of Talmud Torah 3:1). Moreover, he says that whoever dedicates himself to total immersion in Torah "becomes sanctified as the Holy of Holies" (Mishneh Torah Laws of Shmittah and Yovel 13:13). At the *brit* (circumcision) of a child, we offer the prayer that he will grow to "Torah, *chuppah*, and good deeds."

The genuine *Talmid Chacham* is the pride and joy of the Jewish people. He is a teacher, guide, and role model whom all aspire to emulate.

The greatness of the nation resides in the profound respect that it accords to these true heroes of the spirit. Because of our great awe for their wisdom and the behavior it produces, we seek to emulate them and raise our children to be like them. When they die, extreme honor is shown to them. Every Jew then becomes a mourner.

Whom we mourn for reflects our values. When Miriam, Aaron, and Moses died, the entire nation mourned.

This mourning is a form of divine service. It expresses our deep regard for righteousness based on wisdom and *chesed* (kindness). It elevates us to a higher level and strengthens our conviction that the path of the true *Tzadik* is the highest form of life, which we must strive for.

We must be fully cognizant of the implications of this serious matter. The culture that we live in at present does not reflect the moral values that we ought to aspire to. The heroes of American society are not its great thinkers and spiritual role models. Rather it is those who achieve great fame and wealth in sports, cinema and other areas that attract public adulation.

The message that is conveyed to our youth is that what really matters is not the degree of wisdom and personal perfection one attains, but practical success measured by the extent of one's material possessions and public acclaim.

It is important for us to resist the tide and not submit to the worship of society's heroes. We must demonstrate by word and example just how much we value substantial Torah study and the performance of good deeds. And we must display our great respect for people who devote their lives to the virtues and ideals that are truly consequential.

The lives of the great Tzadikim that dwell among us will then provide great benefit for us and even in their deaths, their blessings will endure.

In the Merit of the Righteous

The book of Bamidbar contains many tragedies that had far-reaching consequences. The greatest setback of all was the sin of the spies and the inability of the Exodus generation to fulfill the Divine plan of conquering and inheriting the land.

In addition to this national catastrophe, there were other personal tragedies. Parshat Chukat recounts the death of the three great leaders of the generation: Moses, Aaron, and Miriam. Moses's death doesn't actually occur in this *sedra* (Torah portion), but the sin that sealed his fate, not to enter the land, is recounted here.

We do read of the death of Miriam and Aaron. According to the Rabbis, these most illustrious prophets died by what is known as "death by the kiss" (Talmud Bava Batra 17a). Maimonides explains that they reached the highest level of "love" for Hashem, and this experience was at its most intense as they approached death.

The Torah treats the deaths of Miriam and Aaron differently. Regarding the former, it merely says that the people dwelled in Kadesh, and "Miriam died there and was buried there" (Numbers 20:1). The people's reaction is not mentioned. Was there a period of national mourning, as would have been appropriate? Not a word about this is said.

All we are told is that "there was not water there for the congregation, and they gathered to complain against Moses and Aaron" (Numbers 20:2). This incident led to Hashem's command to Moses to bring forth water from the rock. Moses failed to execute this correctly, thereby losing his right to enter the land.

The juxtaposition of Miriam's death with the absence of water is not accidental. Rashi points out that, during all their years in the wilderness, the Jews had a steady water supply, in the *merit* of Miriam. Now that she was gone, they lost the water.

I believe there is a very important lesson here. We lack a sense of gratitude and appreciation, especially for great *tzadikim*. There was no national mourning for Miriam, because she was not a public personality like Moses and Aaron. She stayed in the background, and perhaps her great deeds were unknown.

Yet without her, *Moshe Rabbeinu* might not have been born. Her courage in staying near the basket where he had been placed, and her quick-thinking intervention with Pharaoh's daughter, enabled Moses to be nursed by his mother, Jochebed.

She and her mother were responsible for defying Pharaoh's order to kill every male child at birth. Miriam was a great prophet and a "hidden" *tzadeket*. There are many people, in every generation, whose lofty level is not recognized because they are anonymous. Their reticence is no excuse for our failure to notice their righteousness.

Chukat

We must develop a sensitivity to true greatness and acknowledge it, so it can become a source of inspiration to all. The removal of the water after Miriam's death was a message that Divine benefit comes because of merit. Had the people recognized that, they might not have complained to Moses about the water.

They would, instead, have asked, how can *we* attain the merit to remain worthy of Hashem's bounty? And that could have opened the door to many unanticipated possibilities.

Do We Respect Other Religions?

Parshat Chukat contains the Law of the *Parah Adumah* (Red Heifer), which is essential to the rite of purification for one who has contracted *tumah* (ritual impurity) through contact with a human corpse.

We no longer have the ashes of this animal and cannot attain the state of ritual purity. However, this does not cause any practical impediments to our spiritual fulfillment, as we no longer have the Temple that, in order to enter, requires us to be *tahor* (ritually pure).

We continue to study the laws pertaining to the Heifer in any case because of the great wisdom they contain. It is also necessary to be learned in these areas, as their performance will be reinstated with the advent of the Messiah, who will rebuild the Temple and, who may come at any moment.

The subject of death pervades Parshat Chukat. In fact, three great leaders of the Jews, Miriam, Aaron, and Moses, meet their end here. Miriam and Aaron actually die in this *sedra*,

Chukat

and Moses's death is decreed here because of his sin by the "Waters of Contention."

Miriam's death is juxtaposed to the exposition of the *Parah Adumah*. The Rabbis, cited by Rashi, found meaning in the connection of these two themes. "Just as the *Parah Adumah* affords forgiveness from sin," they said, "so too does the death of *tzadikim* (righteous people) effectuate atonement" (Rashi on Numbers 20:1).

This idea is both challenging and troubling. At first glance, we can't help but associate it with the Christian doctrine of "vicarious atonement."

Jews harbor no hostility to any of the world religions. We respect the right of all people to embrace the theology of their preference and will not demean them for their religious choices.

However, this does not mean that we regard all the religions as being of equal validity. We believe that the Torah constitutes God's *exclusive* revelation, to the Jews and all mankind.

Moreover, a fundamental teaching of Judaism is that the Torah is eternal and will never be altered in any way. We therefore regard all claims of a "new" revelation that nullifies or distorts any Torah doctrines to be *false prophecy*.

Let us be very clear about this vital matter. There is a reason why our forebears resisted the brutal pressures to convert that were imposed on them by both Christianity and Islam. Our people were steadfast and loyal to Torah, preferring a martyr's death to conversion to a religion they knew to be false.

While certain versions of Islam still regard Jews to be infidels who should be destroyed, major doctrinal alterations have occurred in Christianity. In the aftermath of the

Holocaust, virtually all Christian denominations, Catholic and Protestant, engaged in soul-searching and moral reckoning. They needed to confront the impact of their anti-Semitic teachings in shaping the hateful mindset that made the Holocaust possible. Faced with the horrors of the Holocaust, practically all denominations were forced to revise their teachings about the place of Judaism and the Jewish people. They proceeded to rescind the pernicious belief that God had terminated His Covenant with the Jews. Equally significant, they "absolved" the Jews of the "sin" of "deicide" that had provided justification for the persecution of our People through the ages. In fact, they declared that anti-Semitism is sinful.

Would that they had recognized these simple dictates of reason and decency many, many years ago! This alone could have prevented countless crimes against the Jews and even the Holocaust. Unfortunately, that was not how history unfolded.

We are thankful for the forthrightness which enabled the Church to carry out such a drastic revision of one of its core teachings.

The Jewish policy is to be respectful of all branches of Christianity and seek to maintain appropriate relations with them. However, this does not imply any revision of our historical rejection of Christian theology. We can and must be able to dismiss doctrines we deem to be false, and yet, to respect the dignity of people who adhere to them.

We should be mindful of the injunction of Rabbi Soloveitchik and other rabbinic Sages forbidding religious dialogue with representatives of other faiths. One must appreciate how problematic that would be. If we were to be totally honest, we would have to express how mistaken we regard their doctrines to be, and this could have extremely

Chukat

harmful consequences. It is, therefore, best to assume an attitude of mutual respect without engaging in theological discussion. Neither should we endeavor to "reconcile" the teachings of the various religions.

Rashi's assertion that the death of the righteous constitutes an atonement is deeply problematic. The notion of "vicarious absolution" is a cornerstone of Christianity, which we emphatically reject. How are we to understand this Rabbinic teaching in a manner consistent with our own theology?

In my opinion, there is nothing mystical or magical about the doctrine of the "death of the righteous." It operates in a natural, understandable way.

We often fail to honor great people while they are alive and, consequently, do not learn from them as much as we could. While part of us looks up to and admires truly superior people, there is always an element of resistance to their moral authority. Some of our greatest teachers were not recognized and were even vilified during their lifetimes.

No one illustrates this tendency more than the Rambam. Despite his preternatural genius and piety, he had many opponents who disparaged his monumental achievements. He himself understood that his contemporaries were predisposed to opposition, but that future generations, free of the competitive drive, would recognize the value of his works.

The supreme value of a *tzadik* is not appreciated while he is alive. However, his death has a profound impact on his generation, who now begin to venerate him and investigate his ideas and ideals, which raises them to a higher level. He now assumes the status of a role model and effectuates a genuine *teshuva* in the people.

Do We Respect Other Religions?

This is what the Rabbis mean when they say, "The righteous are greater in death than they were in life" (Talmud Chullin 7b). This profound Torah teaching is unique to Judaism and should not be compared to the doctrines of any other religion.

The Red Heifer

Parshat Chukat describes the ritual procedure of the *Parah Adumah*. The Torah has a unique attitude toward the subject of death. We need to recognize and appreciate the extreme difference between Judaism and the other religions on this matter.

The two other "major" religions, Christianity and Islam, are firmly grounded in man's aversion and inability to accept human mortality. Man faces an intractable conflict between his yearning for eternal life and his inescapable awareness that *this* world is temporal. He has no choice but to recognize on an intellectual plane that, at some point, he is going to die.

But do we truly internalize this truth on an emotional level?

Even at an advanced age, many people initiate ventures that would only make sense if they were to be around for a very long time. Many human behaviors are founded on the unconscious premise that that they will be here forever.

The Red Heifer

To resolve this fundamental dilemma of human existence, people turn to religion, which, for many believers, enjoys immunity from rational scrutiny or the need to make sense.

Under the influence of the "religious imagination," man invents a fantasy of paradise, in which he will exist eternally. This is expressed by the archetypal idea of the "happy hunting grounds." The particulars of the afterlife *vision* may vary with different groups, but essentially reflect their primary values and ultimate aspirations.

Of course, there is a "price" to be paid for admission to heaven. The basic requirement is that one must sacrifice, to a certain extent, one's share in *this* world. For some reason, which is not fully explained, you just can't have it all. You must choose. If you desire the joys of paradise, you must cut back on the delights of this world.

Therefore, the primary motivation of most people in undertaking the restrictions of their religion is to be "saved" from death and awarded immortality.

The most blatant illustration of this type of thinking is the Islamic jihadist. In his view, life in this world is devoid of significance and value. Relinquishing it is seen as a paltry price to pay for the great joys of the afterlife.

This attitude is regarded as a significant advantage in the Islamic war against the "infidel." Islamist terrorists openly proclaim that *we* are at a disadvantage because we cherish life, but *they* love and celebrate death.

Faulty religious doctrine can be the most destructive force on earth. It is only through major theological revision within Islam that the war against terrorism can be won.

What is Judaism's view on this vital subject?

Chukat

Our religion affirms the supreme value of *"tikkun olam,"* perfection of the world. Those who contribute to the betterment of mankind through commerce, scientific progress, and social welfare perform a great *mitzvah*.

According to the Rambam, the commandments have two purposes. First, they convey vital knowledge of the highest truths that are essential to human fulfillment. They are *also* designed to improve our moral nature by instilling ethical virtues and training us to behave with mercy, justice, and love for mankind.

The Torah does not want us to sacrifice life, but rather to joyfully live it on the highest possible level.

That is why the Torah doesn't speak very much about death, which is *not* the focal point of its philosophy. Instead, its aim is to ameliorate the human condition in *this* world for both the individual and society as a whole. We must take note that the afterlife *is* alluded to, but not explicitly mentioned, in Scripture. Judaism emphatically does *not* recognize a conflict between man's enjoyment of life and his quest for eternity.

To the contrary, for the person who lives righteously, there is a seamless transition between this world and the next.

Proper observance of the commandments perfects the soul, enabling the person to have a fulfilling life in the here and now. That is because the course of moderation and rational benevolence prescribed by the Torah is in line with man's nature and leads to personal fulfillment and social harmony. Upon death, the perfected soul continues its existence, and attains an ultimate state of bliss that is beyond our capacity to imagine or describe.

Parshat Chukat introduces us to the concept of *tumah* that is acquired through contact with a human corpse. The most pertinent consequence of *tumah* is the inability to perform the service in the Temple.

The ashes of the Red Heifer, when mixed with water, were used in the purification process, which required seven days. The impure person was sprinkled with this special water on the third and seventh day and, after immersion in a *mikvah* (ritual bath), would regain a state of *taharah* (purity).

Why would contact with a corpse disqualify a *Kohen* (priest) from the Temple service?

I would like to suggest one possible rationale. The type of religiosity that is steeped in the fear of death, and *longing* for immortality, is a corrupt theological approach that is totally antithetical to the ideals and objectives of Judaism.

Encountering a corpse has a sobering and depressing effect on man. It renders him susceptible to religious mechanisms that he hopes will save him from a similar fate.

That is not the state of mind in which a person should approach the true service of Hashem. The Torah wants to *dissociate* the fear of death from the life-affirming values of the Holy Temple.

Our religion extols the "Service of Love" and urges us to worship Hashem with joy and happiness. We should be secure in the understanding that the Supreme Creator, who granted us life, will not take it away from us if we live in the manner He intended for us. May we merit to achieve this.

Death by the Kiss

Parshat Chukat is the *saddest* in the entire Torah. Those of us who cherish *Chumash,* and assiduously seek out its wisdom for guidance, become emotionally attached to its great heroes. They are our mentors and role models, whose noble behaviors we seek to understand and emulate.

Thus, there is a certain sense of loss when we encounter the death of Miriam, who played such a monumental role in our history. Together with her mother, Jochebed, she defied the genocidal decree of Pharaoh against Jewish male newborns, bravely stood watch over little Moses, and boldly convinced Pharaoh's daughter to let her find a Hebrew woman to nurse the Jewish baby. She also led the women in song and dance to give praise to Hashem for the splitting of the Red Sea.

As if her passing were not enough, the lives of her brothers, Aaron and Moses, also come to an end in this *sedra.* Moses doesn't actually die here, but his fate is sealed, along with Aaron's, because of his sin at the *Mei Merivah* (Waters of Contention).

When we read the account of that trespass, it is impossible to comprehend what Moses did wrong. It seems that he and Aaron faithfully executed Hashem's instructions. We only realize that something is amiss when Hashem pronounces the irrevocable punishment for the disobedience. The problem is so completely *hidden* that all of the great commentators are at odds in explaining it.

The fact that there are many conflicting opinions on so vital an issue indicates the severe complexity of this matter. Perhaps we will have more to say on this subject at a different time, but it is outside the scope of this essay.

Parshat Chukat depicts the poignant death of Aaron. Hashem instructed Moses to bring Aaron and his son Eliezer to the peak of Mount Hor. He was to remove the vestments of the *Kohen Gadol* from Aaron and place them on Eliezer, thereby anointing him to succeed his father. Aaron thus had the privilege of witnessing his son's ascension to the most exalted religious position in Israel. Aaron was then to lie down on a special bed that was prepared and his earthly existence was *consummated*.

The Rabbis tell us that Moses greatly desired the same passing as Aaron, which is designated as *death by the kiss*. The Rambam elucidates this phenomenon in his *Guide for the Perplexed*. In general terms, it means that a person who has battled to gain mastery over his instinctual desires and has pursued the delights of knowledge becomes spiritually transformed as he gets older (Guide for the Perplexed, Part 3, Chapter 51:15).

The aging process is, for this person, a great benefit. For as his passions diminish, his convictions become firmer

Chukat

and his love of truth more unshakable. This process culminates with the death of the "kiss." As he experiences the onset of death, his love of God assumes a profound dimension, and he leaves this world in a glorious state. What we call death is actually, for him, the inception of eternal life.

According to our tradition, only three people merited to achieve this exalted experience: Miriam, Aaron, and Moses.

A *midrash* describes a strange occurrence when Moses and Eliezer descended the mountain. "Where is Aaron?" asked the people. Moses told them that he was deceased. The people refused to believe him and said, "Is it possible that the one who stood up against the angel of death and terminated the plague is now overcome by that angel?"

Moses then pled for Divine mercy, and the ministering angels showed the people a vision of Aaron lying on his deathbed. When they saw this, they *believed*. (Midrash Tanchuma, Chukat 17; Midrash Bamidbar Rabbah 19:20).

At first glance, this *midrash* seems very strange. I do not take it literally, but believe it is communicating a significant teaching.

At its core is the idea that the people refused to believe that Aaron had died. Why wouldn't they accept Moses's word, which was supported by Aaron's son, Eliezer?

In my opinion, the *midrash* is based on the awareness that *denial of death* is one of the most powerful human tendencies.

Most people go about their lives under the *fantasy of immortality*. This illusion is nurtured by their identification with certain charismatic figures who seem *immune* to dying. We have all known individuals who seemed so "full of life" that we could not imagine them *not alive*. When these people *do* perish, it is shocking, because we now begrudgingly realize that "if they can die, so must we."

That is why the people refused to accept the fact that Aaron was dead. He was their hero, who had thwarted the angel of death and whom they felt would live forever. As long as they could sustain that belief, they had no need to worry about mortality. Moses prayed that they would be able to accept the truth of the news of Aaron's death and absorb its lessons.

Judaism does not regard death as a tragedy. In fact, one of the Rabbinic interpretations of the verse in Genesis, "And God saw that it was *good*," refers to *the day of death* (Midrash Bereishis Rabbah 9:5).

The notion of human immortality is not necessarily a pipe dream. Our Torah teaches us that we are designed to live eternally. If we adhere to the *mitzvot* of the Torah and appreciate its wisdom, we will be "fortunate in this world and inherit the world to come" (Ethics of Our Fathers 5:19).

May Hashem give us the wisdom to disavow illusions and cling to the *Tree of Life*. Eternal life.

BALAK

Seduction

Those Who Curse

We *Are* Different!

The Power of a Curse

Seduction

Parshat Balak is very strange. The Jews have had no shortage of enemies in their long history, but the one we encounter in this story was very unusual.

Balak recognized that he could not defeat the Jews by conventional means. This is not to suggest that he was overawed by their physical might. The Jews were not a military power in the conventional sense, even by the standards of those times.

What was it about the Jews, exactly, that prompted the great fear of Balak? And what drove him to the unorthodox manner in which he sought to "wage war" against his imagined enemies? For Balak turned to a renowned soothsayer, and not to military experts, in pursuit of his goals.

Yet it is difficult to understand what triggered Balak's fear. The Jews had no designs on his land, nor did they constitute any threat to his power.

Quite to the contrary and unbeknownst to him, Balak had much to gain from Jewish talent and expertise. The Jews are among the most generous people on earth. The Torah records, for example, how Moses pleaded with his father-in-law, Jethro, to join the people on their journey to the Promised Land. Why did Moses appeal to him so fervently? Simply because he wanted Jethro to share in the great blessings that awaited the Jews in *Eretz Yisrael*. Moses said to his father-in-law, "And if you go with us, then that good which Hashem will bestow on us, we will share with you" (Numbers 10:32). Unselfish love of *giving* is a universal characteristic of the Jewish People.

Those who recognize Hashem, and appreciate the blessings that He bestows on man, are inspired by His attribute of goodness and want to emulate it by making His bounty available to others. Had Balak sought to befriend the Jews, he would have been warmly welcomed and embraced. They would have been happy to share their knowledge and wisdom in many areas, and would have provided whatever assistance they could. Balak's tragedy was that he didn't allow himself to get an accurate glimpse of the true nature of the Jews.

What can we learn from Balak's strange behavior?

Balak is typical of many Jew-haters who have disgraced the pages of history. He was motivated by envy of the Jews. He could not get over his jealousy at the fact that they were a special people. He could not bring himself to utter praises of the Jews. All he could say was, "Behold the nation which has come out of Egypt; they have covered the face of earth" (Numbers 22:5).

These few words, "has come out of Egypt," tell it all.

We are tempted to say, "Really? That's it? They just 'came out of Egypt,' a band of slaves that happened to overpower the mightiest kingdom on earth; that's how you

Balak

describe it?" The greatest miracles of deliverance in all of history have taken place, and that's all you have to say?

Balak had to know that the way he phrased it was woefully inadequate to express what had actually happened. He certainly knew that the Egyptians were completely devastated and finally destroyed at the Red Sea, not by any mortal power, but by the Being who is in control of *everything*.

Balak could not come to grips with the unique character of the Jews and their special relationship with the Creator of the Universe. He couldn't tolerate the success of the Jews, and was determined to prevent them from fulfilling their mission to establish *Malchut Shamayim* (Kingdom of Heaven) on earth.

Yet Balak realized that he was powerless to rise against their God. He understood that to defeat his nemesis, he had to discover their spiritual vulnerability and exploit it. His devious notion was to take a different angle of attack: to use the services of Balaam, who, he hoped, would curse them.

Balaam was an evil genius who had the ability to uncover the fatal weakness of any society. Hashem, however, prevented him from uttering these curses, i.e., the hidden secrets that could be used to destroy the spiritual fiber of *Klal Yisrael*. Instead he caused Balaam to pronounce the most beautiful praises, in which he articulated the sublime virtues of this people.

One would think that Balaam's prophetic revelations about the great qualities of the Jewish nation and its exalted historical mission would have had a transformative effect on him. Like Jethro, he should have thanked Hashem and attached himself to Moses and the Jews.

Yet, he did not. At the core, he remained an egomaniac with boundless ambition. Explaining this, Rabbi Israel Chait has said that even the experience of prophecy, of the most exalted kind, cannot rehabilitate a person. Only genuine *teshuva*, beginning with acknowledgment of sin and determination to change, can accomplish that.

Balaam harbored bitterness against the Jews and wanted to bring them down. He knew that Hashem hates promiscuity and idolatry, so he hatched the devilish scheme whereby the daughters of Midian would seduce the Jewish men and thus bring down upon them Hashem's wrath.

The daughters of Midian did as they were instructed and, sadly, the Jewish males were very vulnerable to their amorous inducements. Perhaps it wasn't merely the sexual attraction, as much as the ego boost provided by being the desired object of beautiful, gentile women.

In any event, at the moment of sensual arousal, the women implored the men to join them in their idolatrous ceremonies, and they complied. The punishments that God visited upon His People as a result of their wanton transgressions were very severe.

There is much that we can learn from this today. The strategy of Balak, to harm the Jews by causing them to sin against their God and suffer His retaliation, achieved formidable success. In the contemporary world, especially in America, the barriers between Jews and gentiles have dissipated. One result of this has been a stunning increase in the incidence of intermarriage. The religious dangers that inhere in romantic relationships with non-Jews, which are clearly illustrated by this narrative, cannot be minimized.

We must be vigilant against our many enemies, some of whom sometimes manifest themselves as friends. We must realize that military confrontation is not the only danger we

Balak

face. Our strength resides in our moral integrity and commitment to upholding the holy lifestyle of Torah.

The danger of seduction by hedonistic temptations is greater than ever. Yet we must realize that the Jewish future requires a firm commitment to practice Judaism and an absolute determination to perpetrate it as much as the ability to physically defend ourselves.

Let us dedicate ourselves to cultivating the wisdom, discipline, and moral strength we need to uphold our Torah and to be a leader, not a follower, of the nations.

Those Who Curse

Parshat Balak centers around the idea of blessings and curses. This phenomenon is a major theme of the Torah, which promises great rewards to those who follow God's commandments and punishments for the disobedient.

However, the desire for practical benefits, or the fear of negative consequences, should not be the basis for our service of the Creator. The Torah is a *Tree of Life* (Proverbs 3:18), which should be observed because it is the guide to genuine human fulfillment.

Therefore, we should constantly strive to upgrade our understanding of Judaism and appreciation of the Torah way of life.

When Moses implored God to "Show me Thy ways," he justified the request by saying, "In order that I will find favor in Your sight" (Exodus 33:13). Maimonides deduces from this that Hashem finds *favor* with those who seek to increase their knowledge of Him.

Balak

This fact should be a strong motivation for everyone to *always* pursue a greater understanding of God's Torah. Doing so not only enhances our wisdom and understanding, but renders us more favorable in the eyes of God. We should never be complacent, nor allow ourselves to stagnate in our practice and exploration of Judaism.

Parshat Balak deals with a different type of curse: that which is uttered by man. Balak had witnessed the military conquests of the Jews and wanted to weaken and defeat them. He sought to their undoing by soliciting the services of the renowned soothsayer, Balaam.

This individual had a reputation for being able to achieve outcomes with his *words*. In entreating him, Balak said, "For I know that *who* you bless are blessed, and *who* you curse are cursed" (Numbers 22:6). But we must ask, does any person have the power to produce *unnatural* results by the mere utterance of *words*?

To attribute supernatural powers to any human is idolatrous. No pronouncement made by Balaam could effectuate any change in the natural order. We must firmly believe that all curses enunciated by *people* are completely ineffective.

Yet the Torah *does* prohibit us from invoking the name of God to blaspheme a fellow Jew. This is enjoined because it is a misuse of Hashem's name and an act of hostility against another person, who is psychologically vulnerable and can suffer emotional harm by being the object of harsh vituperation. However, one who is *totally* sound in his belief in God *should* have no concern about other people's thoughts and words.

Had the Jews been at the highest level of understanding and Torah observance, there would have been no need to counter Balak's intention. Balaam's curses would have been entirely ineffectual.

However, the Jews did have weaknesses and defects, and Balaam's evil genius might have detected them and revealed to Balak how he could exploit them. Hashem therefore intervened to protect His people.

This parsha is very relevant to our times. Israel's enemies cannot defeat her militarily, thank God. They have taken to "cursing" her with names, calling her an aggressor, occupier, Nazi, and other insidious epithets. They seek to undermine Israel by depicting her as cruel and immoral, knowing that Jews are very sensitive to these types of accusations.

We should be completely oblivious to the "curses" of these contemporary Balaams. Their filthy labels are a reflection of their own vile character traits, which they project onto the Jews.

But what are we to do? We are human and susceptible to world opinion.

The answer resides in Hashem's warning to Balaam: "Do not curse the nation, for they are blessed" (Numbers 22:12). We are blessed with God's Torah, which is the source of genuine morality. When we study its ideas and live by them, we will *only* be concerned with finding favor in *Hashem's* sight.

Then we will be immune from the wicked accusations of evil people. And we shall become a strong, independent, and great Nation. May we renew our desire to gain greater knowledge of God and His Torah and thereby become worthy of His abiding favor.

We *Are* Different!

Parshat Balak contains a fascinating and usual story that illustrates how Jew-hatred is built into the fabric of reality.

I don't mean to say that people are compelled to hate Jews. Rather, they are predisposed on the emotional level to a dislike of things Jewish. Nevertheless, man has free will and must use his mind to understand and overcome his emotions, however base.

Balak was a Moabite king who was deeply affected by the victories Israel had achieved over two mighty Amorite kings, Sihon and Og. This caused him to solicit the services of Balaam, who was renowned for his ability to bring down people through the medium of his "curses."

What engendered the fear of Israel that consumed Balak? The verse states, "Moab was terribly afraid of the people, for they were numerous; Moab was disgusted because of the children of Israel" (Numbers 22:3). This citation contains two distinct ideas. The first tells us that Balak feared the Jews because they were more numerous and seemingly

We Are *Different!*

stronger than his own people. The second is that, for some reason, the Moabites were disgusted by the Jews.

This *pasuk* requires elucidation. What was it about the Jews that provoked a sense of revulsion, and how is it relevant to explaining the background of Balak's actions?

The Ramban maintains that Balak knew that the Jews had no intention of attacking him. He explains that the feeling of disgust was brought about by all the great miracles that God had performed for the Jews in Egypt and the Wilderness, which Moab had heard about.

One wonders why these acts would produce a feeling of abhorrence. Interestingly, we see the same phenomenon among the Egyptians. The verse states, "And the more they afflicted him, so he increased and so he spread out, and they were *disgusted* because of the children of Israel" (Exodus 1:12). What caused this strange emotional reaction?

In my opinion, the feeling of revulsion is related to a certain distaste and hatred for the Jew. There are many reasons for this. A significant factor is that Jews are *different*. In the *Havdala* blessing we recite at Sabbath's end, we praise Hashem who differentiates "between holy and profane, light and darkness, Israel and the nations." The difference between us and the nations is akin to that between light and darkness. In what sense are we so fundamentally unlike?

I believe the difference is rooted in one's basic approach to life. Every individual and nation lives its life according to the pleasure principle. Most people simply follow the inclinations of the heart in seeking the physical and egotistic gratifications, that are based in the imagination.

The Jew is different. He withdraws from the ordinary pursuits of the world. He acknowledges the Creator in all areas of life and subscribes to a national mission of being a holy

Balak

people. He does not seek renown in any area, but strives to sanctify and glorify the name of God in His world.

Something about the Jew is disturbing to others. It may be a fear that his renunciation of human glory, and adherence to the life of the mind, might actually be a superior form of existence. There is, thus, a desire for the Jew to fail and concede that his approach to life is not workable.

When the Jews are successful, and their numbers increase, it is seen as a grave threat. When they are the beneficiaries of great miracles, it is, simply, too much to bear. The phenomenal growth of the Jews aroused the envy, hatred, and disgust of both Pharaoh and Balak.

Rashi explains what motivated Moab to turn to a soothsayer. He says that when Moab recognized that the Jews were victorious in a manner that was contrary to the natural order, they sought advice from the people of Midian, where Moses had resided. The Midianites said that all of Moses's power was "in his mouth." Moab then said, we too will go up against him with someone whose power is in his mouth (Rashi on Numbers 22:4).

Balaam recognized that the Jews' strength resided in their unique Torah way of life, which secured their relationship with the Creator. Therefore, the king initiated is perverse plan to bring Divine retribution upon the Jews by seducing them into promiscuity and idolatry, which their God "hates." Balaam grasped the full significance of the difference of the Jews, but his disgust with the lifestyle of holiness prompted him to seek their destruction.

There is much we can learn from this story. We must recognize and acknowledge our difference and uniqueness. We should be able to deal with the fact that others dislike and are even revolted by us. If that is because we scrupulously adhere to the requirements of the Torah which God has entrusted to us, we should regard the hatred as a badge of pride. When the criticism of the haters becomes intense let us remember that we *only* need to answer to Hashem.

This does not mean that we should never pay any attention to what the gentiles say about us. If we are being condemned, we need to honestly consider the cause. If it resides in our own unworthy actions or behaviors, we need to correct them, for obtaining a bad name among the nations constitutes a *Chilul Hashem* (Desecration of God's Name).

However, we should never be ashamed about the special position that the Jews occupy in the Divine scheme of things, for this has nothing to do with any innate superiority, but, only, with adherence to Torah and *mitzvot*.

It is our national mission to proclaim God's praises to mankind. We should embrace it with humility, pride and boundless enthusiasm.

The Power of a Curse

Parshat Balak tells the beguiling story of an attempt to bring down the Jews through a strange and unique mechanism.

The people of Israel have been plagued with a never-ending stream of enemies seeking their downfall throughout history. However, the approaches used have varied. Most have sought to afflict the Jews through superior force. The worst example of this is the Holocaust, which surpassed all other onslaughts due to the availability of modern methods of destruction. And yet, Hitler's methods were primitive in comparison with the nuclear technologies that proliferate now.

Iran poses the greatest existential danger to Israel today. It has openly declared, as did Hitler, its intention to annihilate the Jews. If Iran manages to obtain a nuclear arsenal, all bets are off. "The West," which basically means Israel and the United States, must be absolutely committed to preventing this.

Prime Minister Netanyahu has warned that the Iran nuclear deal of 2015 only *postpones* for a few years that regime's march to obtaining weapons of mass destruction. Let us hope that the two democratic allies will have the foresight and courage (as did Menachem Begin) to strike preemptively, if necessary, to disable Iran's genocidal ambitions.

Other Anti-Semite enemies have sometimes employed more subtle techniques, seeking to harm the Jews by seducing them into abandonment of their ideals— specifically the observance of Torah.

One might think such an effort would be an exercise in futility. But history shows that it is not. In fact, it is quite potent. The Greeks almost destroyed Judaism by its lethal process of Hellenization. Many Jews abandoned Torah in favor of the alluring Greek hedonistic lifestyle.

The Maccabees, who arose to rescue authentic Judaism, therefore had to direct their fire against the Jewish Hellenists as well as the Greeks. There are times when brother must fight against brother. Most dangerous is the enemy from *within*, the people among us who hate Judaism and seek its extinction.

The shrewdest of our enemies seek to discover and exploit our inner shortcomings and turn our weaknesses against us. None was more devastating than Balaam, who had keen insight into the fragile psyche of the Jewish people. He realized that they were vulnerable to the *power of the curse*.

The Torah treats the matter of curses very seriously. It is a major Biblical prohibition to use Hashem's name to wish damnation on a fellow Jew, because this is a distortion and a misuse of one's relationship with the Creator.

A curse can also cause terrible harm to the object of the imprecation. The Rabbis warn that we should not take lightly the curse of even an ordinary person.

Balak

Do we believe that mere words have the power to magically secure results? Judaism is categorically opposed to any and all forms of superstition. Indeed, whoever attributes supernatural powers to a mere mortal engages in idolatry, because he attributes divine power to a temporal being.

Curses actually can cause harm but that is *only* because of human psychological weakness. We are vulnerable to the condemnation of others if we assess our worth by what people think of us. This is one of many reasons to shun all forms of *lashon harah* (slanderous speech).

Although the desire for approval is one of the most powerful motivational forces in human life, it contains enormous danger. There are very few truly great leaders in the world today, though not because there is a dearth of people with knowledge and political skill. Rather, the crucial element of *civil courage* is lacking.

Every great leader must be able to take actions and stake out positions that are unpopular, but are essential to the wellbeing of the people.

Most leaders, however, are overpowered by their need for approval. Very few have the fortitude and self-confidence to follow the truth no matter how despised and rejected it may be.

As Jews, we trace our origin to *Avraham Avinu* (Abraham our Forefather). His absolute commitment to the truth of his conception of Hashem and his willingness to defy all of mankind in proclaiming his unique religion were distinctive and unparalleled.

Abraham was also known as *Avraham HaIvri*. The Rabbis explain the meaning of the term *Ivri* (Hebrew) as meaning "All the world was on one side, and Abraham was on the other side" (Bereishis Rabbah 43:8).

Today, our enemies use weapons of physical destruction, as well as hatred and social condemnation, against us. They criticize us as being immoral and even compare us to the Nazis. Unfortunately, many Jews are negatively affected by those who spew hate and have a distorted sense of morality.

We must reaffirm and strengthen our identification with our Forefather Abraham. We must rededicate ourselves to the truth of Torah and not be affected by the curses of wicked people who hate us irrespective of what we do.

Should we seek and be concerned about obtaining approval? Yes, we should. We should be absolutely focused on being worthy of *Hashem's* approval. If we are deserving of that, then human attitudes will be of no significance.

May we merit to walk proudly and confidently in the ways of Hashem with joy and confidence.

PINCHAS

Indifference of the Righteous

Religious Zealots

The Hedonism of the Times

The Righteous Zealot

Righteous Revenge

A Prophet of Their Own

Why Did Elijah Despair?

Indifference of the Righteous

Parshat Pinchas begins with a special reward that Hashem dispensed to Phinehas, "His covenant of peace" (Numbers 25:12). Rashi explains that this phrase refers to the priesthood. The ultimate objective of the *Kohen* and the priestly service is to establish peace in the midst of *Klal Yisrael*.

Until this point, Phinehas had not obtained the status of a *Kohen*. Originally, Hashem designated Aaron and his sons to be Kohanim, as well as their *future* descendants. That is to say, the original designation only pertained to the sons of Aaron alive at the time, and to the grandsons of Aaron who would be born from that point on. Phinehas, who was the son of Elazar, son of Aaron, was already living at the time that the priestly status was conferred by Moses and, therefore, did not receive the status of *Kohen*.

Thus it was only now, and as a reward for his heroic deed, that Hashem conferred upon him His covenant of peace, whereby he was rendered a *Kohen*.

The question arises, what is the nature of this reward, and what connection does it have to Phinehas's deed?

Phinehas took matters into his own hands and executed summary justice against the prince of the tribe of Shimon. This person, named Zimri, was openly consorting with a Midianite princess named Kazbi bat Tzur. Phinehas caught them "in the act" and executed them without the benefit of any due process.

At first glance, the action of Phinehas seems problematic and contrary to ordinary civil norms. It certainly does not appear to be related to the objective of peace, which is the lofty goal of the *Kohanim*. How are we to understand this strange phenomenon?

Moreover, one of the first teachings in *Pirkei Avot* is to "be patient in judgment" (Ethics of Our Fathers 1:1). This is primarily intended as advice to judges: that they should not adjudicate on the basis of preconceived notions, but should put emotion aside and deliberate slowly and carefully. The decisions they reach should be the result of a full process of objective analysis and not an instinctive "gut" reaction.

That is clearly not the manner in which Phinehas responded to the scandal that confronted *Klal Yisrael*. He reacted instantaneously, with great decisiveness and courage, in executing two major figures. And his deed was so great that it found supreme favor with Hashem, bringing an end to the plague that had decimated the ranks of the Jews.

Thus we see that the injunction of the Rabbis to go slow in judgment does not apply to *all* cases. Life doesn't always provide us with the luxury of investigating matters from

Pinchas

every angle. Sometimes a person *must* have the ability to recognize what constitutes a true catastrophe and to deal with it immediately. Such was the case with Phinehas.

The breakdown of sexual morality that he confronted was the result of a devious plot that had been concocted by Balaam. He wanted to destroy Judaism from within, by having the Midianite women seduce the men into sexuality and idolatry.

In addition to being a severe moral breakdown, this constituted a public desecration of Hashem's name, the worst aspect of which was the failure of anyone to do anything about it. The indifference of the righteous to transgressions of the wicked is a great sin.

The "anger" of God flared against the people, and a severe plague broke out that consumed many. Phinehas recognized that this was not a time for deliberation, but for action. He could not bear the desecration of God's name by the people whose mission was to sanctify it.

With clarity and inspiration, he remembered the teaching that everyone else had forgotten: that one who engages in the behavior of Zimri may be dealt with by *zealots*. Phinehas's actions were thus not motivated by personal anger, but by his zealousness for the honor of Hashem, which was being sullied.

Matters such as these which severely desecrate the name of God do not allow for any hesitation. The one who is imbued with an authentic love of Hashem and a willingness to risk everything for His sanctification-- and that person alone-- is qualified to "avenge the insult." Phinehas was such a person. As a reward, Hashem granted him His covenant of priesthood.

The task of the *Kohen* is to promote real, not phony, peace. This can only come about when people recognize God and submit to His will. This condition is necessary because true peace demands the clarity to recognize evil and the courage to destroy it in the name of Hashem.

The greatness of Aaron, the first *Kohen*, was that he was a man of the people who "loved peace and pursued peace" (Ethics of Our Fathers 1:12). He sought to resolve interpersonal conflicts, especially those between husband and wife. He was extremely creative in this endeavor and was prepared to sacrifice his own honor, if necessary, to establish harmony in human relationships.

At first glance the social mission of Aaron would seem to preclude the summary execution of sinners, as Phinehas did with Zimri and Kasbi bat Tzur. Such a harsh action would run the risk of causing the *Kohen* to lose his popularity with the people.

However, the true peacemaker must be able to put aside personal feelings when necessary and do that which is objectively essential for the spiritual health of the nation, no matter how startling his act may seem at the time.

A dedicated parent must at times be able to bear the angry reaction of his child and administer a harsh but absolutely required punishment. A parent who is incapable of experiencing the momentary condemnation of the child cannot properly fulfill his task.

So too, the *Kohen* who is charged with tending to the spiritual needs of the Jewish nation must be dedicated to the practical welfare of every person and be willing to do everything possible to maintain social harmony and *shalom*.

But, he must also realize that *true* peace cannot ever result from catering to people's emotions and avoiding actions that will elicit their disapproval. His goal must be to always consider the ultimate state of their souls. For only when the

Pinchas

nation is in a state of actual spiritual health can *genuine* peace be established.

May we be worthy to be blessed with courageous and dedicated leaders like Aaron and Phinehas.

Religious Zealots

Parshat Pinchas describes the reward that Hashem granted to Phinehas because of his great and heroic deed. A plague had broken out, destroying thousands of Jews who had sinned in the matter of worshipping the idol *Baal Peor*.

Balaam, the Gentile prophet, had been prevented from uttering curses against the Jews. Instead, he had been inspired to pronounce wonderful blessings upon them. However, even an exalted prophetic experience cannot reform a sinner. Balaam did not choose to recognize and overcome his moral defects, and soon reverted to his sinful self.

Balaam had an overriding need to inflict harm on the Jews, and he did so using a unique and unprecedented strategy. All the great enemies of the Jews refused to acknowledge that the Jews were, in fact, God's chosen people; had they recognized the special relationship between Hashem and the Jews, presumably they would have desisted from their antisemitic designs.

Pinchas

Except for Balaam. He knew without doubt that Hashem had chosen the Jews, and he wanted to provoke Him into punishing them. According to the Sages, he reasoned that "the God of this people hates promiscuity" and would severely afflict them if they indulged in it (Talmud Sanhedrin 106a).

Balaam's cynical advice to the Midianites was to exploit the Jews' vulnerability to Divine punishment. He suggested that they send forth their attractive women to lure Jewish men into sexual relationships. That alone would have been bad enough, but he went further. The Midianite harlots were instructed to up the ante by prevailing upon their Jewish lovers to join them in their primitive idolatry of Baal Peor.

This devious strategy had lethal consequences, as a large number of Jews were soon ensnared in the dual sins of immorality and idolatry.

Balaam's anticipation of Divine punishment proved to be prescient. A plague that killed thousands descended upon the Jews. Hashem instructed Moses to execute justice against all who had sinned, and that would cause the punishment to cease. As Moses set himself to the task at hand, a new calamity occurred. It is one thing for ordinary people to engage in sinful behavior, but when respected leaders do so, it can have devastating results.

A prince named Zimri, of the tribe of Shimon, was openly consorting with a Midianite princess named Kazbi. This was a public *chilul Hashem* and required immediate action.

At once, Phinehas entered the tent of the lovers and slew them. He was acting under the statute, "Zealots may deal with him" (Rashi on Numbers 25:7). In certain cases, the Torah permits a genuine zealot to execute summary justice without recourse to ordinary legal procedures.

Righteous Zealots

This parsha is very relevant to current events. Religious zealots, especially those who murder in the name of God, have rightfully gotten a bad name among decent people. We decry the horrible actions of fanatics who commit the worst atrocities in the name of God. In 2014, for example, we were all distressed at the news that some Israeli teenagers murdered an innocent Arab child in revenge for the terrible execution by Arab terrorists of the three Jewish martyrs, Eyal Yifrach, Gilad Shaer, and Naftali Frenkel, *Zichronam L'Bracha* (May their memories be a blessing).

Parshat Pinchas, however, extols Phinehas's zealotry and precipitate action. What differentiates the righteous zealot is that his sole motivation is to defend the honor of God and to terminate the desecration of His name. Phinehas's action was directed at the true culprits, *while* they were engaged in the deed, and served to glorify God's name. The alleged Israeli teenaged avengers, in contrast, took an innocent life and desecrated the name of Hashem and the Jewish people. Their actions could only incite the Palestinians to further acts of violence and thus to further endanger Jewish life.

Hashem rewarded Phinehas by elevating him to the priesthood and granting him His covenant of peace.

Religious zealotry is a double-edged sword. If it is rooted in one's baser instincts, it can be used to inflict great harm on others. The case of Phinehas shows that there is also a form of zealotry that is rooted in the pure love of God and in the desire to magnify His name. When utilized in the proper context, it can bring great benefit to the world.

Let us strive to cultivate a *genuine* zeal for the service of Hashem.

The Hedonism of the Times

Parshat Pinchas begins with the sanctification of Phinehas as a *Kohen*. This honor was bestowed on him as a special reward for his heroic deed.

There is nothing more detestable to the Creator than when His chosen people descend into idolatry and immorality. We are supposed to be a special nation distinguished by its affirmation of the true God of reality, its embrace of a life of *kedusha*, and its absolute negation of idolatry.

The evil sorcerer, Balaam, had been hired by Balak to curse the Jews. Hashem prevented him from doing this and, instead, made him the instrument through which the most beautiful praises of Israel would be expressed.

Hashem gave Balaam the gift of prophecy, and his words were recorded in the Torah.

One would think that this would have been a transformative experience for him. After perceiving all the wonderful things that were destined for the Jewish nation, we are amazed that Balaam did not follow the example of his fellow Midianite, Jethro, and join them.

Yet there was a fundamental flaw in Balaam's character. The beautiful visions he beheld did *not* impact his soul. He still desired to follow the dictates of Balak, who had summoned him to curse the Jews, in order to make it possible to drive them from his territory.

Due to Hashem's absolute prohibition, Balaam was unable to accommodate him. However, his failure to satisfy Balak's request disturbed him. Because he needed recognition and approval, he came up with a devious plan to damage the Jews.

Balaam knew a thing or two about Judaism. He understood that the God of the Jews hates immorality. He also realized that, if the Jews could be enticed into idol worship, they would be vulnerable to the Almighty's retribution. Balaam understood the power of lust and sexual seduction.

He crafted the scheme to have the Moabite women offer their sexual favors to the Jewish men and thereby lure them into the worship of the idol known as Baal Peor.

It was only because Balaam was so steeped in sensuality that he was able to conjure such a plot. Indeed, his lack of personal holiness was the flaw that prevented him from becoming a truly great prophet. But his plan worked, and, in punishment, a plague broke out, taking the lives of 24,000 sinners. During the plague, a Jewish tribal leader consorted with a Moabite princess, and they were publicly flaunting their relationship. Phinehas assumed the role of a righteous zealot who, in circumstances like this, are permitted to "deal with" the sinners. He had the courage to risk public condemnation for the sake of sanctifying God's name, and slew them both. Phinehas's deed was so great that it ended the plague.

Pinchas

Phinehas reaffirmed the fundamental character of the Jewish people as one that abhors immorality. Throughout history, the Jews have been distinguished by their modesty and family purity. A life of sexual lust and hedonistic indulgence is contrary to our national mission to be a "kingdom of priests and a holy nation" (Exodus 19:6).

This lesson has great relevance for contemporary Jews. The world around us is divesting itself of traditional morality. The governing principle is that there is no absolute moral right or wrong. Everyone must have the freedom to pursue their own instinctual gratification and to engage in any form of carnal behavior, no matter how grotesque it may appear to more refined souls. The mantra of the sexual revolution was "do your own thing," and all forms of gratification are good, as long as "nobody gets hurt."

Judaism maintains that the essence of man is the divine soul, and sensual craving stems from the physical, animalistic aspect of his nature. Our life's task is to perfect our soul and to master our impulses. We do this by employing discipline to satisfy our desires in a rational and constructive manner. This is the path to holiness.

The purpose of sexuality is procreation. Man's carnal impulses must be gratified in the framework of marriage, whose chief purpose is to have and raise a wholesome family. Judaism is therefore categorically opposed to the Supreme Court's badly misguided decision to render gay marriage a constitutional right. This is categorically in opposition to the Torah position which is clearly stated in the Book of Leviticus (18:22).

Jews must not be seduced by the hedonism of the times. We must proclaim the truth to Jew and gentile alike. We need to remind everyone of the Biblical commandment to "Be holy, for I, the Lord your God, am holy" (Leviticus 19:2).

The Righteous Zealot

Parshat Pinchas describes the enormous reward Hashem granted this man for his great deed. A plague had broken out among the Jews because of the terrible sin into which they had been *ensnared*.

The Midianites, with the collusion of Balaam, had come up with a diabolical plan to wreak havoc on the Jewish people. Rather than confronting the Jews in open warfare, they sought to destroy them from within.

What is amazing is that their strategy presupposed belief in the truth of Torah, particularly its teaching that God holds the Jews to account for their sins.

There are no greater transgressions than idolatry and sexual licentiousness. The Midianites reasoned that, if Jews could be lured into these behaviors, they would place themselves at serious risk for Divine retribution. The plan was to use the Torah as a weapon with which to slay the Jews.

This was truly an astounding phenomenon that runs contrary to ordinary human psychology. Generally, if a person

The Righteous Zealot

becomes convinced of the truth of a religion, his desire is to *observe* it. But these sinners acknowledged Hashem and His Torah, and *still* sought to subvert His will by instigating His people to rebel against Him.

This attitude reflects a unique type of evil never seen again in history. It reinforces the warning that we must guard the secrets of Torah, lest they fall into the wrong hands. For many oppressors have arisen with the intention of forcing us to abandon Judaism and to eliminate our religion from the world. The Midianites never imagined, on their own, that by causing us to sin, they could arouse God's wrath against us. That plan would have required that they acknowledge the veracity of Torah, something they could not bring themselves to do. Only through Balaam's advice were they guided to bring the Jews to sin. Thus we must take care not to communicate information about the Jews, that can be turned against us, to hostile actors.

As a result of their sin, the Jews were smitten with a severe plague.

Hashem told Moses to appoint judges and execute justice against all who had engaged in the idolatry of Baal Peor. Only in this manner would the plague be halted.

But suddenly, the disaster took on a new dimension. The prince of the tribe of Simon participated in the sin when he openly flaunted his affair with a beautiful Midianite princess named Kazbi.

It's one thing when ordinary people transgress, but quite another when great leaders shamelessly violate the most sacred tenets of Judaism.

Phinehas did not hesitate. He sprang into action, remembering the teaching that, in public desecrations of this kind, "zealots may deal with him" (Rashi on Numbers 25:7).

Pinchas

He entered the tent of cohabitation and put a spear through both of them. As a result of this great deed, the plague, which had consumed 24,000 people, was halted.

Phinehas was a righteous zealot. However, at first sight, his action requires further elucidation.

In our time, the label "religious zealot" has gotten a bad reputation. Today, Islamic Jihadists react with murderous anger at any perceived insult to their "prophet" or religion. Anyone who publishes an article or cartoon that can be seen as disrespectful to Islam puts his life in grave jeopardy.

We roundly condemn that attitude and view it as depraved. Thus, it behooves us to ask, what is so noble and different about the action of Phinehas?

The answer is that the average person identifies with his religion and its icons. If it is insulted, he takes it as a severe *personal* affront. He may not admit it, but it is his personal anger which motivates his need for revenge.

This person is generally a hateful and disgruntled character, totally lacking in human compassion. He is not acting for the sake of noble ideals, but hides behind them so he can unleash his great subjective frustrations and resentments.

We must therefore be very honest about our emotional reactions to perceived offenses against our religious convictions. Do we feel bad because of our intense attachment to certain moral ideals? Or is it so bothersome to us because we take it as a *personal* insult and therefore need to take revenge.

The truly righteous zealot must be a person on the highest level of wisdom, love, and compassion. His zealous deed does not emanate from a selfish, emotional disposition. He acts *only* because of his great love of Hashem and his complete absence of rancor towards anyone -- because he recognizes the great harm caused by a blatant desecration of God's name.

This type of zealot seeks the peace and well-being of mankind, and, like Phinehas, deserves to be a *Kohen* and initiated into Hashem's "Covenant of Peace."

Let us strive for that ideal.

Righteous Revenge

Parshat Pinchas describes the great reward that was bestowed on that unique individual, who performed a great deed during the unfolding of Balaam's devious plot.

Hashem had warned Balaam in no uncertain terms that he was not to do as King Balak had requested, but was only to utter the words that Hashem "placed" in his mouth (Numbers 22:35). It thus transpired that instead of denouncing the Jews, Balaam expressed the most beautiful blessings and envisioned the great future that awaited the chosen nation.

He had been thwarted from fulfilling Balak's wish that he "curse" the Jews to weaken them, and his failure to do so earned him no favor. The King was furious that the devious prophet had done the opposite of what he desired.

However, Balaam got his revenge against the people he had been compelled to bless. His outlandish scheme was to destroy the Jews by using their religion against them, maneuvering them into behaviors that would bring Hashem's "wrath" upon them.

Righteous Revenge

Tragically, his plan worked. He urged the Midianite and Moabite women to sexually seduce Jewish men to entangle them in idolatry. After the Jews indulged their sexual appetites, they subsequently became attached to the worship of the idol Baal Peor. As anticipated, Hashem's "anger" was kindled, and the Jews were punished with a terrible plague.

What type of person was Balaam?

We generally encounter two kinds of people in Scripture, the good and the bad. Where does Balaam fit in? He received prophecies so magnificent that they were included in the Torah, verbatim. How could a person who reached that level stoop so low? How could someone experience the most exalted prophetic insight and then descend into the most blasphemous behavior?

Balaam was gifted with unique capabilities. The Rabbis say, "The greater a person is, the more powerful are his inclinations" (Talmud Sukkah 52a). Balaam had a great desire for wealth and fame. His challenge was to master his formidable instinctual drives and tremendous psychological energy and to dedicate himself to the service of Hashem.

Judaism maintains that there is no such thing as a *tzaddik* (righteous person) *by nature*. All our great leaders and prophets were endowed with powerful drives. King David was a mighty warrior who possessed supreme courage and skill. He *chose* to sublimate all his energies to the service of Hashem.

David personified the Rabbinic dictum that one should serve God with his good *and* "evil" inclinations (Mishnah Berachot 9:5). He used his great military prowess to fight the holy wars that protected Israel and made the building of the Temple possible.

Yet, he is remembered not for his conquests, but for the Psalms he composed, which are read to this day by Jews

181

Pinchas

and even members of other religions who seek spiritual enlightenment and inspiration.

Although Balaam had great talent and was granted a profound prophetic experience, he did not work on perfecting himself. The Rabbis say, "Greater is the one who conquers his inclination than the one who captures a city" (Proverbs 16:32). He did not engage in heroic battle with his own nature. In the end, he was conquered by his basest emotions.

Contrast Balaam with Phinehas, who faced a singular challenge. The seduction of Jewish men extended to the highest echelons. Zimri, son of Salu, openly consorted with a Midianite princess and brought her into his tent. All the onlookers were stunned and paralyzed.

Except for Phinehas. He did not hesitate, but dispensed instant vengeance for this public desecration of God's name. He was not intimidated by the lofty position of the sinners, but entered the tent and, catching them in the act, thrust his spear through both of them. He put aside all fear of man and acted solely for the sake of Hashem. Hashem rewarded Pinchas with His "Covenant of Peace," the status of a *kohen*.

Why would an act of violence warrant a gift of peace?

The significant teaching here is relevant to our own times. The world today suffers from an excess of misplaced "tolerance." The failure to avenge what is truly evil only encourages continued wicked behavior and demoralizes those who seek to be righteous.

There are times when our love of Hashem and desire to sanctify His name demands the ability to eschew restraint and unwarranted mercy and to visit violence on the guilty.

Of course, this must be done only by people of the highest moral character who, alone, are qualified to be genuine "zealots of Hashem." It is only by wreaking vengeance against the genuine enemies of Hashem that true peace will come.

That is why Pinchas was appointed a *kohen*, whose ultimate purpose is to bring peace to the Jewish people and to the world. We should be aware that weakness, masquerading as *compassion,* can bring about terrible upheaval and suffering. The fearfulness and self-deception of Western leaders prior to World War Two emboldened Hitler and encouraged his aggression. After capitulating to that dictator's humiliating demands they boldly proclaimed that they had preserved "peace in our time."

Instead the world suffered the most destructive cataclysm in human history which included the Holocaust. True peace *could* have been attained but only by a "zealot" like Phinehas who would recognize genuine evil and know how to deal with it. May his bold example serve as an inspiration to contemporary world leaders who have the enormous responsibility of keeping the world safe in the nuclear era.

A Prophet of Their Own

Parshat Pinchas tells the story of a great hero whose *zealous* action for the sake of Hashem's honor halted a terrible plague afflicting the people.

All this happened because of the effectiveness of Balaam's wicked plot. He sought to undo the Jews by bringing them into severe disfavor with their God. He knew that the Ruler of Israel hates lewd promiscuity, especially when it is connected to idolatry.

Balaam, therefore, counseled that the Midianite women should embark on a campaign to seduce Jewish men into sexual relationships that would then give them the leverage to entrap the victims in worship of their idols.

The plan worked and produced catastrophic results. Divine retribution came about in a plague that ravaged thousands. It got so bad that Zimri, prince of the tribe of Shimon, audaciously and publicly consorted with Kazbi, the daughter of a Midianite ruler named Tzur.

A Prophet of Their Own

Phinehas rose to the occasion, *remembering* Moses's teaching that, in public desecrations such as these, "Zealots may dispose of him" (Rashi on Numbers 25:7). He entered the tent of cohabitation and put a spear through both of them.

Phinehas overcame all fear and acted purely for the sake of heaven. His deed found favor with Hashem, Who rewarded him with His *Covenant of Peace*. Through this covenant, Phinehas assumed the status of a *Kohen* and, throughout the history of the Temple, many of his descendants occupied the position of *Kohen Gadol*.

It seems ironic that Balaam, who had reached such heights of prophetic inspiration that his pronouncements were deemed worthy to be included in the Torah, should be the author of such a perverse plot. According to the Rambam, a true prophet must be on the highest level of moral, ethical, and intellectual perfection.

Because of this, many commentators do not regard Balaam as a great prophet in the traditional sense. Rather, Hashem caused His spirit to *rest* upon him and inspired him to utter beautiful prophecies, even though, on his own, he would not have merited this distinction.

According to Rashi, Hashem granted a revelation to Balaam to divest the *nations* of an excuse for *not* accepting the Torah. They might have said, "If we had our *own* prophets, we would have returned to the *good*." Hashem, in His infinite mercy, granted them a prophet of their own (Rashi on Numbers 22:5).

In my opinion the nations' argument was not logical, but emotional. The great prophets of the Jews, beginning with Moses, were messengers to the *entire* world.

Pinchas

The story of Jethro is instructive. He clung to Moses, learned from him, and eventually converted to Judaism. He didn't need a "prophet for the Gentiles."

Jethro's behavior reflected the true Jewish position on these matters, which is that one should "Hear the truth from whoever speaks it" (Maimonides, Introduction to *The Eight Chapters*). The Rambam studied the works of the great thinkers of the nations, including Aristotle, who, he said, achieved the highest level of intellectual perfection short of prophecy.

In my opinion, which is based on extensive experience, this is *not* the governing principle in many contemporary Jewish academic circles. When someone expresses a new theory on a significant matter for consideration, the reflexive response is, "Where is it written?" or "*Who* said that?"

Many competent Torah scholars will accept an idea because of the stature of its author, even if it is subject to disagreement. For example, if a group is involved in a lively discussion on some theological topic, and someone suddenly announces that the Rav (Rabbi Joseph Soloveitchik) said such and such on that matter, this will, inevitably, terminate the discussion. For after the Rav has spoken, what need is there to say more? This is a widespread phenomenon, even if the idea presented is problematic and open to challenge.

There is no doubt that the Rav was a great Torah genius whose words should be treated very seriously, but misplaced *awe* of authority can stifle true intellectual maturation.

A genuine *talmid chacham* should strive to develop his mind to be capable of *independent* thought. Only by virtue of this can he truly benefit from the voluminous body of Torah wisdom that constitutes the intellectual heritage of the Jewish people.

The *inalienable* right and duty of man to use his own mind has its source in the Torah. It depicts both Abraham and Moses questioning a Divine decree and being *vindicated*. When Hashem informed Moses that He would destroy the Jews because of the Golden Calf, Moses vociferously argued against that. He subjected Hashem's "position" to a logical critique and demonstrated its negative consequences and, as it were, "dissuaded" the Creator from carrying out His intention.

The notion that man can challenge Hashem, disagree with Him and, indeed, even "win" the argument is an astounding concept that no other religion maintains or is even aware of.

Of course, Hashem doesn't *actually* change His mind. But he does enable man to reach a higher level of understanding by giving him the opportunity to confront the Master of the Universe on an intellectual level.

In granting man this privilege to come before Him in debate, Hashem affirms the *validity* of human reason and reveals the full consequences of the verse in Genesis: "In the *image* of God created He man, male and female created He them" (Genesis 1:27).

The nations of the world did not use their independent judgment and carefully study the teachings of Moses and the numerous other Jewish prophets. They needed to hear it from a *prophet of their own*. This precipitated the elevation of an imperfect person who used his genius for nefarious purposes.

We must maintain profound respect for great thinkers and masters of wisdom. But we must not surrender our capacity for independent thought. We are always responsible to think for ourselves, to the best of our ability. And that is

Pinchas

why we should heartily pray to Hashem to mercifully grant us knowledge, discernment, and good sense. For only thus can we become true servants of Hashem. May we merit to achieve this.

Why Did Elijah Despair?

The Haftorah for Parshat Pinchas recounts the story of the prophet Elijah. Like Phinehas, he was a man who exhibited "zealousness for Hashem." In fact, there are Rabbis who are of the opinion that "Elijah, he *is* Pinchas" (Rashi on Bava Metziah 114b).

Elijah was a *navi* (prophet) in the days of King Ahab and Queen Jezebel. Unfortunately, they were wicked leaders who sought to entrench the nation in the idolatrous worship of *Baal*. They succeeded in executing most of the genuine prophets of Hashem, who were replaced by the false advocates of *Baal*.

Elijah convinced Ahab to gather the entire nation at Mount Carmel, where he put the false prophets to a test—and they totally failed. He then called upon Hashem to send down a fire to consume the sacrifice that he had offered. The subsequent miracle had a profound impact on the people, who proclaimed, "Hashem, He is the Lord" (I Kings 18:39), the chant with which we conclude the Yom Kippur services. All

Pinchas

of the phony soothsayers who ministered to Baal were then executed.

This auspicious moment should have initiated a widespread return to the service of Hashem. Elijah, seemingly reconciled to the king, accompanied him on the trip home to Jezreel, running before his chariot as a display of honor.

The momentary euphoria did not last long. Ahab told Jezebel what had happened at Mount Carmel, and she was furious. She sent word to Elijah that in a short time, he would meet the same fate he had visited upon her "prophets."

Elijah ran off into the Wilderness, where he beseeched Hashem to take his life, for "I am no better than my fathers" (I Kings 19:4). In response, Hashem told him that He would "meet" him at Mount Sinai.

A remarkable dialogue took place at that encounter. Hashem said, "Why are you here, Elijah?"

To which he replied; "I have been exceedingly zealous for Hashem, God of Legions, for the Children of Israel have abandoned Your Covenant; they have razed Your altars; they have killed Your prophets with the sword, so that I alone have remained, and they seek my soul to take it."

And Hashem said, "Go forth and stand on the mountain before Hashem; and behold!—Hashem is passing, and a great, powerful wind is smashing mountains and breaking rocks before Hashem—but not in the wind is Hashem; and after the wind an earthquake—but not in the earthquake is Hashem; and after the earthquake a fire—but not in the fire is Hashem; and after the fire a *still, thin sound*" (I Kings 19:9-12).

After saying that Hashem was not to be found in the mighty forces of nature, the verse mentions the "still, thin

Why Did Elijah Despair?

sound" without defining its character. How are we to understand Hashem's response to Elijah's dilemma?

If God's intention was to express His displeasure with acts of zealousness, why did He support Elijah with the miracle at Mount Carmel that led to the slaughter of the prophets of Baal? And why was Phinehas rewarded with the "Covenant of Peace" in exchange for his violent action against the sinners?

We need to understand why Elijah suddenly descended into despair after the great miracle at Carmel. He was so uplifted by that amazing event that he ran before Ahab's chariot to personally honor the king.

In my opinion, his mood went into a tailspin when he received the threatening message from Jezebel. His depression was not because he feared death, for that is precisely what he requested from Hashem. Rather, his hope that the miracle would bring the people back to the true worship of Hashem was now dashed.

He recognized that he would need the king's support to achieve a national religious renaissance. He truly believed that Ahab was moved by the great miracle he had himself witnessed and would become an ally in restoring the nation to the service of Hashem. That is why he joined him on his return journey and displayed such great respect.

However, his worst fears materialized. He knew about the influence that Ahab's idolatrous wife had over him, but he thought that the king, who was otherwise a powerful leader, could follow his independent judgment when he was convinced of the truth.

Unfortunately, Elijah now had to acknowledge that the king was totally controlled by his wayward wife. Ahab *should* have threatened Jezebel to renounce Baal worship or face severe consequences. But he could not bring himself to do it,

Pinchas

and this meant that the goal Elijah had set for himself in the miracle at Mount Carmel would not be attained. This extreme frustration impelled him to entreat Hashem to terminate his prophetic mission and end his life.

In His final message to Elijah, Hashem "clarified" the virtue of zealousness, which is of great value when used in the proper context. Phinehas's zealousness ended the plague which had been brought on by the licentious behavior of those who had been seduced by the Midianite women.

So too, the miracles performed by Elijah on Mount Carmel were dramatic and inspired the people to assert that Hashem is the true God and to slaughter the false prophets. But miracles, no matter how powerful and earthshaking, may have only limited consequences. They were certainly not enough to transform Ahab into a person who could overcome his emotional dependency on Jezebel's approval.

In His revelation to Elijah, Hashem showed him that, while demonstrations of massive power are sometimes necessary, they are insufficient to fulfill the Divine mission on earth. Miracles are required at times to remove evil forces that block the path of true morality, but on their own, cannot produce significant and lasting change.

That can only be achieved by the "still, thin sound." The transformation of mankind will only come about through genuine *education* based on calm, clear reasoning without any extraneous compulsions.

Elijah's story is very relevant to our lives, especially to those who devote themselves to *tzorchei tzibbur* (the needs of the community). There is a great temptation to "complete the task," which often impels us to resort to pressures of various kinds. And, indeed, there are situations which do require the courage to suspend ordinary constraints and act with "boldness."

However important that may be, it must constitute the exception, not the rule. We should never be tempted to resort to power, physical or emotional, as a means to achieve the religious commitments we want people to have.

An illustration of the interaction between compulsion and comprehension can be found in the Talmudic statement that at Sinai Hashem held the mountain over them like a vat, and proclaimed that if they accepted the Torah it would be fine, but if not, this would be their burial place (Talmud Shabbos 88a). The Rabbis thus asserted that an element of force was necessary to "persuade" the Jews to accept the Torah.

However, that is not the end of the story. The Talmud goes on to say that at the time of Purim they reaccepted the Torah out of love. That is because they were then able to observe the superiority of the Torah life style and its profound wisdom as manifested in the heroic deeds of Mordechai and Esther.

As we study Jewish history, we must realize how significant the force of the "mountain hanging over them" has been in preserving Judaism. Can Judaism survive in an environment of total acceptance and assimilation like that of contemporary America? Is our love of Torah sufficient to enable us to resist all the allures of contemporary society which are now ours for the taking?

We are still in need of external pressures that impel us to embrace Judaism. But we pray to Hashem in the words of King David, "Open my eyes that I may perceive the wonders of Your Torah" (Psalms 119:18). We must cultivate the capacity to understand and communicate the profound ideas of Torah in a rational, intellectually compelling manner that

Pinchas

will enlighten the minds and inspire the hearts of all with whom we interact. Then we can finally be released from the "mountain" which has hung over us to protect us for so long, so that we may serve Hashem and keep His Torah faithfully out of profound appreciation and love. May we merit to achieve this.

MATOT-MASEI

Dealing with Chutzpah

Fatal Attraction

Mean What You Say

Excessive Religiosity

Sometimes Anger Works

Judaism is the Answer

Dealing with Chutzpah

The book of Bamidbar concludes with the reading of its final two *parshiot*, Matot and Masei.

In general terms, reading Sefer Bamidbar is a gloomy experience. It begins on a high note, describing the construction of the *Mishkan* and its dedication. The entire nation was then organized for the triumphal march into the Promised Land. However, from out of nowhere, calamity struck.

A spirit of rebellion took hold of the people, and a series of tragedies ensued. The culmination was the sin of the spies and the decree of the 40-year stay in the wilderness. The tragedy was that the generation who experienced the Exodus and the subsequent miracles of Hashem was deemed unworthy to enter *Eretz Yisrael*.

We can't help but be affected by the plight of the generation of the Exodus. They signify the phenomenon of "missed opportunities" and teach us that not everything in life is *"bashert"* (destined to be). Hashem had intended for the former slaves to be redeemed and take up residence in the Land of Israel. That was what was "bashert."

Yet man has the ability to undo the "intended" and deny himself, through sin, the great benefits that Hashem has prepared for him. That is a major lesson we need to learn from the story of the spies.

Bamidbar also details the events that occur after the 40-year period of wandering. Once again, the people were getting ready to resume the delayed journey to the Land. They had defeated the mighty kings, Sihon and Og, and had inherited their land. Thus, they were now in possession of the territory on the eastern side of the Jordan River, which today is known as the Kingdom of Jordan.

Suddenly, the leaders of the tribes of Reuben and Gad approached Moses with a special request. Both of these tribes had large amounts of livestock. The newly conquered lands were vast and filled with grazing areas that would render them prime property for these people. They requested that Moses allow them to take their inheritance on these lands and not cross the Jordan with their brothers.

Moses responded to them with a sharp rebuke. Although Moses was the most humble and compassionate leader, he could be brutally honest and critical when necessary. He lashed out at the representatives of the two tribes and accused them of undermining the morale of their brethren, who would attribute their decision to settle east of the Jordan to fear of the inhabitants of the Land. This would have dire consequences for the objective of conquering *Eretz Yisrael*.

To hammer home his point, Moses recounted for them the sin of the spies and went so far as to accuse them of being a group of sinful people who have taken up the role of their fathers in arousing the anger of Hashem against Israel.

Matot-Masei

The "offending" parties regrouped and returned to Moses with an entirely new proposal. They would build shelters for their animals and houses for their families. Then they would join their brothers in the war of conquest and be in the vanguard of the military attacks. They would remain on the western side of the Jordan until the conquest was complete, and the people had been settled in their inheritance. Only then would they return to their homes on the other side of the Jordan.

Moses completely reversed his attitude as a result of this extremely forthcoming offer. He formalized the terms of the agreement and warned these tribes to be scrupulous in fulfilling them. What had begun as a harsh and angry confrontation concluded in a peaceful and agreeable manner.

What lesson can we learn from this fascinating account? Moses's initial response seems to be unnecessarily harsh and accusatory, especially in light of the subsequent reasonableness of the two tribes. Why was Moses so scathing and biting in his criticism?

It may be difficult for us, in this age of political correctness, to feel comfortable about Moses's behavior. However, the lesson of the story is that there are times when we need *painful rebuke*.

The two tribes had displayed great insensitivity to the implications of their initial request. They became focused on their personal material needs and lost sight of how their proposal would affect *Klal Yisrael*.

Moses deemed that this obliviousness to the danger of repeating the sin of the spies warranted a reaction that would shake them from their complacency. He was more concerned with the state of their souls than with ruffled feelings. He therefore displayed a side of his nature that we had not seen before, i.e., the ability to deliver a sharp and precise rebuke that shook a person to the core.

There are times in a person's life when one needs a good dose of incisive and piercing rebuke. We should have the courage to deliver it when necessary and to receive it when deserved. For, as the Torah attests, "The one whom Hashem loves does He rebuke" (Proverbs 3:12).

Fatal Attraction

Parshat Matot presents unique challenges to the modern reader. One feels that we simply may not be mature enough to get its point.

The parsha contains the final installment of the inexplicable story of the descent of the Jews into the worship of the idol named Baal Peor. This was a primitive cult whose manner of worship was too disgusting to describe in these pages. In many ways, this episode of idolatry was worse than the Golden Calf.

Matot describes the revenge Moses took against the Midianites who had seduced the Jews into idol worship.

This national disaster resulted from a strategy hatched by the Gentile prophet Balaam. God had elevated him to the highest level of prophetic insight, and he pronounced the most beautiful blessings on Israel.

However, even the most exalted spiritual experience cannot transform a person morally, unless he internalizes its lessons. To become righteous, one must confront his defects

Fatal Attraction

and make strenuous efforts to correct them. After experiencing the heights of prophecy, Balaam reverted to his old self. His desire was to inflict harm on the Jewish people.

Balaam was dangerous because he was an evil genius. He believed that the Jews were God's chosen people, and that therefore, a frontal assault on them would fail. His idea was to cause the Jews to behave in a manner that would elicit God's wrath instead. He knew that "the God of this people hates promiscuity" and would punish His people severely for indulging in it (Rashi on Numbers 31:16).

Balaam advised the Midianite leaders to send forth their beautiful women to entice the Jewish men into sexual relationships. The ladies were instructed to persuade those men who were attracted to them to join in their idolatrous observances. This ruse worked with astonishing success, and a Divine plague killed the 24,000 Jews who committed the dual sins of immorality and idolatry.

Balaam was executed for devising this nefarious scheme. However, the skillful seduction to which they were subjected did not excuse the sinful behavior of the Jews, who had been commanded against cohabiting with foreign women.

What caused them to stumble so badly, and what lesson can we learn from this tragedy?

The great Biblical commentator Sforno elucidates the faulty thinking of the men who were seduced into idolatry. The Torah prohibited intermarriage, warning that it would lead to idol worship. The sinners denied that this concern applied to them. They rationalized their behavior saying that they could have sexual relationships with these women and *not* be drawn after their idolatrous practices. They convinced themselves that they could indulge their sexual desires and still refrain from the pagan practices of their lovers. This proved to be a tragic error.

The Torah is based on the deepest understanding of human nature. You cannot observe Judaism properly if you are romantically involved with someone of a different religion. When you are in love with a person, you will inevitably be influenced by his or her values and religious beliefs.

Parshat Matot contains many lessons. We should respect all the commandments and never second-guess the Torah or try to find a way to work around it. The Jewish way of life is based on discipline and self-control in the gratification of instincts.

Even the sexual drive becomes sanctified when used in the service of God. We are prohibited from marrying Gentiles *not* because they are bad, but because doing so seriously compromises our ability to lead a truly Jewish existence.

Life's most intimate and meaningful relationship should be experienced with one who shares your values and religious convictions. One requires a committed Jewish spouse to properly observe and perpetuate Judaism.

Together, the Jewish couple can build a beautiful home that incorporates the wisdom, compassion, and love that are the hallmark of the Jewish lifestyle. Children raised in this environment are likely to embrace and sustain the heritage that is their birthright.

This is an especially important teaching for contemporary Jews. In the era of assimilation there are many individuals who are still interested in learning about their Judaic heritage and perpetuating it to some extent. However, they also feel very comfortable cultivating relationships with non-Jews and see in this no contradiction to the goal of maintaining a "traditional" lifestyle.

However, this position needs to be carefully analyzed. Our resolve to practice Judaism and raise our children in our traditions is beset by many challenges in the current secular climate. It requires the support and commitment of the *entire* family unit. A spouse of a different religious background cannot be counted on to provide the dedication needed for this goal. Compatibility of values, especially religious ones, is a vital component of a fulfilling marital relationship. And it is absolutely essential to maintaining a harmonious family life. May we merit to achieve it.

Mean What You Say

The *parshiot* Matot-Masei complete the fourth book of the Torah, Bamidbar.

The first subject discussed in Matot is that of vows. Importantly, no one is under any obligation to take oaths or vows upon himself. He should approach this matter with the utmost seriousness.

This is because a Biblical vow is different than an ordinary verbal commitment or promise. Although there is a popular saying that "promises were meant to be broken," we should strenuously seek *not* to be among those to whom this observation applies.

Indeed, we should be mindful of another slogan, "A man's (or woman's) word is his bond." What a person says has great significance. Yet we often speak out of turn, under the sway of powerful momentary emotions, and issue guarantees that are beyond our ability to fulfill. We are then forced to walk back our declarations and suffer the blows to our integrity.

This takes place in many areas of life and causes unnecessary pain and annoyance.

Unfortunately, it is a prominent feature of the *shidduch* (matchmaking) game. People express interest, say they will call or want to "go out" but, in fact, don't really mean it. They lead people on, and thereby tamper with their emotions.

This type of behavior also occurs in other areas of social interaction. People say things that they don't mean. They want to see you, they intend to call you, and so on; the list is endless. They seek to score points with pleasant words that they have no intention of fulfilling.

We should seek to avoid dishonest words such as these and instead strive to adhere to the dictum, "Say little and do much" (Ethics of Our Fathers 1:15).

Of course, we are only human, and sometimes, with the best of intentions, we will make commitments that, subsequently, become extremely burdensome to fulfill.

Are we bound to promises sincerely made without a full awareness of their complexity?

Of course, there are legitimate ways to be absolved of such obligations. However, we should walk the extra mile and strive to be true to our word, even in the most demanding circumstances.

The matter is more serious when we take a formal vow or oath. The verse says that when one takes a vow "unto Hashem," he may not "defile" his word, but must do all that he has said (Numbers 30:3). For when a person swears by Hashem, it is no longer just a matter of being true to his word.

Matot-Masei

The veracity of his belief in the existence of Hashem is at stake in this type of vow. Failure to abide by it involves a desecration of God's name.

That is why we should take pause before assuming an oath, for by doing so, we become vulnerable to dire consequences.

That said, what is the purpose of the institution of vows? Aren't there already enough religious obligations, Biblical and rabbinic, that we are bound to observe? Aren't these sufficient to ensure our spiritual wellbeing? Why would we need to make vows?

The answer, in my opinion, is that the Torah is the best religious system for mankind at large, but individual circumstances vary. For example, bad nutrition or overeating is harmful, but the Torah did not present a detailed list of what to eat and what not to eat. This would not have made sense as, for example, high cholesterol foods like eggs may be bad for some people, but very beneficial for others. The same holds true for excessive caloric intake.

The Torah instructs us about the great importance of maintaining good health, in a general way, but leaves the specific choices to us. Yet the fact is, unfortunately, that many humans are challenged in regulating their appetites and, over time, become "addicted" to dangerous habits.

We know that we must desist from tobacco, alcohol, or maybe our favorite ice cream, but sometimes find that we have lost the willpower to do so. We have allowed our instincts to overpower us, and we are now at their mercy.

At such a time, we need Divine imperative to help us keep our instinctual desires in check. Therefore, the Torah allows us to create, as it were, a new *mitzvah* targeted to our specific needs.

By uttering a vow, one transforms a permitted activity, which was extremely dangerous, into a prohibited one. Or one may swear an oath to perform the exercise that his doctors have said is vital to his very survival but which he has been too lazy to do.

He is now bound by Divine commandments that are specifically addressed to his most essential personal needs.

Many major lessons are contained in this discussion of vows. Perhaps none is more significant than the charge to live according to the principles of truth and honesty and to seek to always be faithful to our word. We should remember that in virtually all of our relationships with significant others as well as the community, the virtue of truthfulness is of paramount importance.

There are certain moments in life when you need people to believe you and trust your word. Yet someone whose record in this area is not spotless will encounter resistance. For people will wonder whether you can be trusted now. At such moments the person whose integrity has been impeccable will reap the benefits of enjoying the confidence of others. One who is scrupulously committed to the truth will find favor "with Hashem and with people" (Proverbs 3:4). May we merit to attain this.

Excessive Religiosity

Matot and Masei conclude the fourth Book of Moses, Bamidbar. Matot begins with a series of laws pertaining to vows.

This is a most complicated aspect of Judaism. In effect, a person can create new mitzvot for himself. He can through, the mechanism of an oath, prohibit something the Torah permits. He can also obligate himself to perform an action that Hashem did not ordain.

At first glance, this seems strange. Jews are governed by 613 commandments, both positive and negative. In addition, we are obligated by numerous Rabbinic ordinances and communal customs that have developed over the long course of Jewish history.

Being an observant Jew is a full-time occupation. Without intending any disrespect, I think it is fair to ask, don't we have *enough* mitzvot? If only we were sufficiently dedicated to keep them all in a meaningful and meticulous manner!

Excessive Religiosity

In fact, making oaths would seem to go against the statement in Psalms 19 that we recite on Shabbat morning, "The Torah of Hashem is perfect, refreshing the soul" (Psalms 19:8). Why would a supreme Law need to be supplemented by individuals' additional "legislation"?

The Torah is perfect in a general sense, both for the individual and the community. However, particular needs vary, and the Torah cannot address every problem of every specific person.

For example, the Torah regulates our eating habits, but only in a general way. While it prohibits certain classes of animals, fish, and fowl, it leaves a wide variety of choices for our indulgence.

Numerous permitted foods are perfectly fine for some people, but deadly for others. Jewish cuisine tends to favor certain dishes that are high in fats; some people can thrive on this food, but it can be a disaster for those with high cholesterol.

We live in a time of great material abundance, and serious health problems can arise from defective eating habits that lead to obesity and disease. Why do people consume foods that harm them? Why do they eschew exercise when they have been told how vital it is to their well-being?

It may sound strange but I believe it is because *nothing* prevents them from engaging in these unhealthy behaviors. The Torah did not specifically outlaw an extra portion of dessert, or even two or three of them.

Of course, there is a general mandate to guard one's health, but the details are left to individual discretion.

Human beings are fragile creatures who are very vulnerable to temptation. No one should frown upon or make light of others' weaknesses. Each of us should look within and

Matot-Masei

acknowledge that there are areas where we simply lack *any* self-control.

The Rabbis insisted that people not expose themselves to temptation. For example, they forbid seclusion between a man and woman who are sexually prohibited to each other.

The Torah recognizes that there are certain things a person can resist *only* if they are Divinely prohibited. When someone takes a vow to refrain from, or to perform, a certain action, the matter now assumes the status of a biblical commandment.

While vows have great utility and can help a person overcome a bad habit (like smoking), there is also a negative aspect. At times, a person may feel overcome with zeal and go overboard in assuming obligations that are beyond his capacity. Eventually, it becomes clear that he took too much upon himself. Yet he is under the obligation of the oath he uttered.

The Torah, which only has our best interests at heart, provides a remedy. One can visit a *Beit Din* (religious court) of three observant Jews and have the vow nullified. The Torah never allows us to crawl into a hole from which there is no escape.

The laws of vows and their nullification contain an important lesson. Just as we sometimes overindulge our physical appetites, we tend to engage in *moral excess*es as well.

In religion, there is also a tendency to do more: to pray more, learn more, visit the sick more, and so on. In certain circles, there a culture of guilt that extols people who sacrifice their own pleasure for the sake of others.

I regard this as the "Mother Theresa" mentality, which asserts the notion that if we discount our own needs enough, live totally for *others*, and renounce all bodily pleasures, we will attain eternal life.

Excessive Religiosity

That understanding does not represent the philosophy of Judaism. We must be rational and intelligent in serving Hashem and should *not* simply copy what others do. Our learning, praying, good deeds, and community service must be commensurate with our individual nature and capabilities.

Also, we should not renounce the pleasures of *olam hazeh* (this world). It is *not* a *mitzvah* to suffer. Rather, we should avoid extremes, of overindulgence as well as abstention, and remember that we must be in the best physical and emotional state to serve God properly and with joy.

Let us remember the words we utter as we return the Torah to the Ark: "Its ways are ways of pleasantness and all its paths are peace" (Proverbs 3:17).

May we merit to observe the Divine commandments with wisdom, psychological insight, and great sensitivity, to bring peace and joy to this world and to prepare us for life eternal.

Sometimes Anger Works

The *parshiot* Matot-Masei, which complete the Book of Bamidbar, record an encounter between Moses and the leaders of the tribes of Reuben and Gad. These two tribes possessed large flocks of animals and needed vast expanses where they could comfortably graze.

Great success can bring unanticipated problems. Quite fortuitously, the Jews had taken over the verdant lands on the eastern side of the Jordan. This happened because the mighty kings Sihon and Og had gone to war against them, only to be roundly defeated.

The governing principle at that time was that *aggression has consequences*. This means that if you embark on war against another country, you run the risk of losing *your own*.

This truth is relevant today, as Israel faces international opprobrium focused on the accusation that she illicitly "occupies" "Palestinian land" in the West Bank.

The entire assertion is baseless, because *all* of the land in question did *not belong to any people* prior to the Six Day War of June 1967. At that time, the territory in question was controlled by Jordan. They had seized it by force, without any legal sanction or significant international recognition, and they were the *actual* occupiers.

Jordan foolishly joined with Egypt and Syria in the '67 war, intending to destroy Israel. Fortunately, Israel prevailed and conquered *all* the lands that Jordan had seized in 1948. Israel has a *right* to the lands that she obtained via a legitimate act of self-defense. In addition, we should remember that this land had no legitimate *owner*; hence, the concept of occupation is not applicable.

The leaders of Reuben and Gad came before Moses and presented their case. They wanted to take their inheritance on the eastern side of the Jordan and forfeit any portion on the western side, as that would be more beneficial to their circumstances.

Upon hearing this, Moses became uncharacteristically furious and subjected them to a severe tongue-lashing. He accused them of being sinful people akin to the *spies*. That group had brought tremendous suffering upon the people and caused the entire generation to wander and die in the Wilderness.

And now, said Moses, you deign to do the same thing? For the people will interpret your maneuver as an attempt to avoid the difficult battles of the conquest and settlement of the land. And their spirit will be shaken.

Moses's harsh rebuke had a sobering effect on the petitioners. They took his words to heart and returned with a proposal. The tribes of Reuben and Gad would leave their families and animals behind in protected areas and join their brothers in the vanguard of the battles that would be fought for the conquest of *Eretz Yisrael*. They would remain until the

Matot-Masei

entire land was divided among the tribes. Only then would they return to their families.

This offer found favor with Moses, as it effectively neutralized his objection. He formalized the agreement and instructed the leaders to deal with the two tribes according to its terms.

This incident seems to be one in which reason prevailed, and legitimate concerns were successfully resolved. But why did Moses get so angry at them in the first place? Couldn't he have calmly explained his concerns and asked if they were willing to make the necessary modifications? Moses was the *most* humble person, and anger was far from his nature. What triggered his biting condemnation?

In my opinion, he regarded the *selfish* behavior of Gad and Reuben as an expression of *poresh min ha-tzibur* (separating oneself from the community). The Rambam maintains that this is a very serious transgression that can cause one to lose his place in *Olam HaBa* (the World to Come).

What does this sin consist of? According to the Rambam, it occurs if a person performs all the *mitzvot*, but does *not* regard himself as a member of the Jewish people. For example, if he doesn't join with them in their joys and sorrows and does not perform *mitzvot* with them, but separates himself and acts as though he is part of a *different* nation, he is guilty of this violation.

This should be a sobering thought, especially when Matot and Masei are read in synagogue: immediately prior to the Fast of Tisha b'Av, which commemorates all the fearsome tragedies of our history. We must be concerned about the welfare of the *entire* Jewish people, not just our own particular group or sect. The well-being of *every* particular Jew, no matter where he may be, is intertwined with that of all the members of the *tzibbur* (group).

Gad and Reuben's initial approach displayed an absence of concern for the impact their actions would have on the emotions of the people in the other tribes. They were only interested in one thing: how will this plan be beneficial to *us*? They failed to consider how it would affect the others' morale.

Moses's timely rebuke brought them back to their senses. They came up with a new proposal that would provide for their own needs and accrue to the benefit of the nation as well.

During the season of national mourning leading up to Tisha B'Av, and all year round, we need to internalize this lesson. We must preserve a sense of *connection* with and *concern* for the entirety of *Klal Yisrael*. We must seek to harmonize our personal desires with those of the *tzibbur*. The *entire tzibbur*.

Judaism is the Answer

The final two *parshiot* in Bamidbar, Matot-Masei, describe the war of revenge that Moses fought against Midian at Hashem's behest.

The purpose of the battle was to exact punishment for the terrible evil the Midianites had perpetrated. They instructed their women to lure Jewish men into sexual relationships. When the seductive women had the men in the grip of desire, they would initiate them into the worship of Baal Peor, a form of idolatry that most people would find revolting.

This diabolical scheme was hatched by the sorcerer Balaam. He discovered a new method of defeating the Jews, which no one before or since has ever conceived. In fact, Balaam was an "evil genius." According to Rashi, he believed that the Jews could not be conquered by superior military forces. He said, "Even if you gather all the nations of the world, you will not be able to defeat them" (Rashi on Numbers 31:16).

Judaism is the Answer

It wasn't that Balaam regarded the Jews as supermen. He understood that their strength came from God, who had chosen them to be His people. He knew that, as long as the Jews had a favorable relationship with Hashem, they would be invulnerable to attack.

But what if he could cause a rupture in that relationship? Balaam knew that "the God of the Jews detests lewdness" and that if they could be lured into sinful behavior, they would be destroyed by their own Protector (Talmud Sanhedrin 106a). Balaam caused great harm, but did not foresee that Phinehas's heroic deed would stem the tide of destruction.

Balaam's tactic has never been repeated. Throughout history, all our enemies have sought to destroy us physically. However, Balaam's methodology, to annihilate the Jews from within by divorcing them from Torah observance, has reared its head in a strange form.

A famous Jewish philosopher once said that the Christians made a major mistake by seeking to convert the Jews through persecution. When you oppress the Jews, they become more defiantly committed to Judaism. He suggested that, if the gentiles would offer great freedom to the Jews and accept them with friendship and love, they would obtain a different result.

The contemporary American experience demonstrates that his contention was accurate. No society has been kinder to the Jews than America. We enjoy freedom of religion, unlimited economic opportunity, and entree into every social and political institution. How has this affected our religious life? Sad to say, in a disastrous fashion.

The Pew report shows that American Jews are assimilating and intermarrying at a prodigious rate. The greatest threat to the future of Judaism comes from within. We have sustained the assaults of every external enemy. Will we, finally, destroy ourselves?

It is incumbent on us to demonstrate the true beauty, rationality, and relevance of Judaism to contemporary life. There is a huge void in the American materialistic, hedonistic lifestyle, and people are searching for meaning. We must be able to show clearly and convincingly that Judaism is the answer.

An illustration of this would be in the area *addiction*. Many of today's problems stem from the inability of people to control their physical and emotional cravings. Our society suffers tremendously from the drug culture which is a fixture of its sensual and hedonistic lifestyle. This produces great suffering for individuals and society at large.

The teachings of Judaism are very relevant and consequential to this matter. Especially significant is the category of *Kedusha*. This lofty ideal requires that we train ourselves to reign in our instinctual drives in all their manifestations. According to Maimonides, we are not supposed to repress our carnal needs, but to gratify them with discipline and moderation.

In this era of unlimited abundance, the challenge for man is to learn how to gratify his appetites in an intelligent and beneficial manner and not become addicted to unlimited and uncontrollable indulgence. The Divine mandate to "Be Holy" is of great relevance to modern life and can, in many cases, spell the difference between life and death.

Many of us may be reluctant to take this "plunge" because we have made such attempts in the past and have failed. So we lost confidence in our ability to make and keep a commitment to the prescriptions of Judaism.

Bamidbar teaches us that we are all imperfect beings who make many mistakes and experience setbacks on the road to meaningful living. Hashem does not want us to despise ourselves or linger excessively on the missteps of the past. The great heroes of the Torah were not without flaws. Some made very substantial errors but did not allow themselves to be destroyed by them.

For example, King David committed a serious sin with Bathsheba. He had great regret and forthrightly acknowledged his transgression. But he did not quit the arena. He remained "King David" and fulfilled his responsibilities. He continued to serve God with vigor and confidence.

We should learn from the examples of our spiritual role models. We should retain our optimism in spite of the fact that we have fallen short in the past. For "It is a tree of life for all who grasp it, and those who uphold it are happy" (Proverbs 3:18).

Judaism is a treasure trove not only of religious observance but of profound wisdom applicable to all areas of life, as well. Let us strive to impart its teachings in an enlightening and inspiring manner.

May God grant us the ability to be exemplars of Jewish life and to model our faith in the most appealing fashion to our brothers and sisters, and to all mankind.

Glossary of Hebrew Terms

Bashert- destined to be
Am Kadosh- Holy Nation
Amidah- petitionary prayer
Aseret HaDibrot- 10 Commandments
Avraham Avinu- Abraham our Forefather
Avraham HaIvri- Abraham the Hebrew
Baal Peor- an idol worshipped by the Midianites
Bechavruta- learning partners
Bechor- the first-born male in a family
Beit Din- religious court
Beit HaMikdash- Holy Temple
Brisker Method- a conceptual method of Talmudic analysis
Brit- circumcision
Chag- holiday
Chametz- leavening
Chesed- kindness
Chesed shel emet- compassion of truth
Chilul Hashem- Desecration of God's Name
Chumash- The Five Books of Moses
Chuppah- marriage canopy
Derech eretz- decent manners
Dvar Torahs- Torah articles
Efes- nothing
Eretz Yisrael- the Land of Israel
Eved Hashem- servant of God
Galut- Exile
Ger- convert
Hakarat hatov- gratitude
Halacha- law

Halachic- legal
Har Habayit- Temple Mount
Hashkafa- philosophy
Havdala- prayer and blessing recited to separate between the Holy Sabbath and the weekday
Hitnatkut- withdrawal (as in, from Gaza)
Ivri- literally "on the other side." See *Avraham HaIvri*
Kedusha- Holiness
Kehuna- priesthood
Klal- community
Klal Yisrael- community of Israel
Kohanim- priests
Kohen- priest
Kohen Gadol- High Priest
Kotel- Western Wall
Lashon hara- literally, "evil speech," i.e., slanderous speech
Luchot- Tablets
Maamad Har Sinai- Revelation at Mount Sinai
Machloket- unnecessary strife
Maggid Shiur- Instructor of Talmud
makchish magidehah- denigration of her transmitters, i.e., teachers of Torah
Malchut Shamayim- Kingdom of Heaven
Matan Torah- giving of the Torah
Mei Merivah- Waters of Contention
Meit mitzvah- literally, *the deceased regarding whom there is a mitzvah.* Someone who passes away with no next-of-kin relatives to bury him
Menahel- educational director
Mesorah- Oral Law
Midbar- desert
Milchemet HaChaim- the battle of life

Mishkan- Tabernacle
Mitonenim- depressed and extremely *discontented* people
Mitzvot- Commandments
Moreinu- Our Teacher
Moshe emet v'Torato emet- Moses is true and his Torah is true
Moshe Rabbenu- Moses Our Teacher
Moshiach- the Messiah
Nachat- satisfaction
Navi- prophet
Nazir- one who has taken a vow of abstinence
Nezirut- institution pertaining to the laws of a Nazir
Olam HaBa- the World to Come
Olam hazeh- this world
Or Lagoyim- light unto the nations
Parah Adumah- Red Heifer
Parsha- portion or section (of the Torah)
Parshiot- plural of Parsha
Pirkei Avot- Ethics of Our Fathers
Poresh min ha-tzibur- separating oneself from the community
Rambam- Maimonides
Ramban- Nachmanides
Rebbe-Talmid- teacher-student (as in "Rebbe-Talmid relationship")
Safsuf- rabble
Sedra- Torah portion
Sefer- religious work
Shalom Bayit- family tranquility
Shechina- Divine Presence
Shidduch- matchmaking
Sotah- Suspected woman
Tahor- ritually pure
Tallit- prayer shawl

Talmid chacham- Torah scholar
Tanach- scripture
Techelet- special blue dye used on a *tallit* fringes
Teshuva- repentance
Tikkun olam- perfection of the world
Torah miSinai- Torah from Sinai
Torat Moshe- the Torah of Moses
Tumah- ritual impurity
Tzaddik- righteous person
Tzadikim- righteous people
Tzibbur- group
Tzizit- fringes worn on a four-cornered garment, such as a *tallit*
Tzorchei tzibbur- the needs of the community
Yam Suf- Sea of Reeds
Yerushalayim- Jerusalem
Zichronam L'Bracha- May their memories be a blessing